Out of Old Manitoba Kitchens

Christine Hanlon

MacIntyre Purcell Publishing Inc.

MacIntyre Purcell Publishing Inc.
194 Hospital Rd.
Lunenburg, Nova Scotia
B0J 2C0
(902) 640-3350

www.macintyrepurcell.com
info@macintyrepurcell.com

Printed and bound in Canada by Friesens.

Design and layout: Alex Hickey
Cover Design: Lloyd Nauss

Hanlon, Christine, author
     Out of old Manitoba kitchens / Christine Hanlon.

ISBN 978-1-77276-052-1 (hardcover)

        1. Cooking, Canadian–Manitoba style–History.
2. Cooking–Manitoba–History. 3. Frontier and pioneer life–Manitoba. 4. Cookbooks. I. Title.

TX715.6.H357 2017   641.597127   C2017-901751-9

MacIntyre Purcell Publishing Inc. would like to acknowledge the financial support of the Government of Canada and the Nova Scotia Department of Tourism, Culture and Heritage.

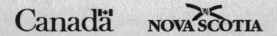

For Francis,
my inspiration in the kitchen, and in life.

Table of Contents

Introduction

Corn on the cob. Crisp and tender, salty and sweet. I love biting into a fresh ear of corn, glistening with butter.

But that wasn't always the case. When I first came to Canada at the age of five and a half, even the smell of corn turned my stomach. My mother always said that back in France, corn was pig food. Back then I was too young to know there were different types of corn.

Today I wonder how, when my great-grand-parents came over from Brittany in the 1920s to homestead near Swan River, they reacted to the tastes of their new homeland. Had they located to a more Francophone area, they would have had the familiarity of crèpes before Lent and taffy on St. Catherine's Day. Instead, thanks to their Ukrainian and Indigenous neighbours, they learned to enjoy bannock at tea time and paska at Easter.

Manitoba owes its rich culinary heritage to its people and the diversity they brought to our kitchens. From the Indigenous peoples to the Selkirk Settlers to waves of immigrants from Iceland and Eastern Europe, families and communities have gathered around the fire and table, keeping traditions alive through the food they served. Instinctively, they knew that preparing traditional food is essential to preserving a culture.

Why else when making the trek across the sea, would the Highland Scots have bothered to pack something as heavy as their precious querns, the Mennonites, their waffle irons, the Ukrainians, their iron grates? Today, as Manitoba's Indigenous peoples reconnect with their cultures, food plays a fundamental role.

After all, cooking and consuming food is central

to all our lives, and not only because we have to eat to survive. A dinner, a picnic, an afternoon tea – this is the common bond that brings us together as a community. The opportunity to share dishes prepared with pride and patience, cuisine that reflects our history and identity, remains central to our shared experience.

While writing this book, I had the privilege of delving into the history of those people who shaped a menu that is distinctly Manitoban. I spent many hours in old Manitoba kitchens at heritage sites, and many more hours in modern kitchens listening to the descendants of the early inhabitants share memories of their ancestors.

I would like to acknowledge all those who contributed stories and recipes to this book. At the same time, I am grateful to the archivists, librarians and curators, who tend all those repositories of documents that would otherwise be lost. Thank you for your invaluable assistance.

This has been a most delicious journey, one that, like a good meal, has left me with a deep sense of satisfaction. We are so fortunate to live in a province that benefits, now more than ever, from the influence of such a wide variety of cuisines. During my research, I asked myself repeatedly what dishes and foods set us apart from the rest of the Canadian culinary landscape. As such, I have tried to focus on those that have had the most enduring influence.

I also decided to limit the scope of influence to the 1920s, as many of my sources indicated this period was a watershed, when canned goods and commercially-prepared foods began to flood store shelves, line refrigerators and sizzle on electric stoves. In addition, most of the large cultural groups that have influenced our collective cuisine were already in Manitoba by then.

In no way does this humble collection presume to encompass all the influences on the food we enjoy in this province, but hopefully you will recognize your own experience through these pages. Consider this a taste of the cookery we call our own. I hope that reading this book will be like savouring a big warm slice of Manitoba!

— Christine Hanlon, Winnipeg, Manitoba

The Food

Breads, Breakfast and Bannock

"Good bread is a necessity for both rich and poor." –
Ogilvie's Book for a Cook (1905)

Although wheat, flour and bread were unknown to the Indigenous peoples of Manitoba, they were a staple for the first settlers and the European immigrants who followed. Initially, the Hudson's Bay Company shipped flour from England to its forts and posts in Rupert's Land. Company men hailed mainly from Scotland's Orkney Islands, where 'bannock' referred to the round shape of a loaf more than to its composition. Soon their Indigenous wives were substituting bison marrow and fat for lard or butter, as bannock's popularity spread among the Indigenous population and the Métis.

Upon their arrival, the Selkirk Settlers had neither lard nor butter, nor the means to buy them, and yeast was completely unavailable. So initially, bread meant a bannock of flour and water, until cows could be raised to provide cream for butter. Soon, the settlers replaced expensive HBC store flour with wheat from their own fields, ground with hand-mills or 'querns' they brought with them from Scotland. The construction of wind and water-powered grinding or grist mills followed. The first windmill built by a millwright was sent from Scotland by Lord Selkirk in 1825. But when it arrived – in pieces – no one knew how to put it together!

Sourdough starter

Once local milling became more readily available, attention turned from making bannock to baking bread. The first leavening agent was sourdough starter, a homemade fermented leavening agent made from potato water, sugar and flour. Then, with the arrival of commercial yeast cakes from St. Paul, Minnesota, in the 1850s, bread-making exploded.

The Icelanders favoured their own varieties of bread, starting with rye because it was the easiest crop to produce in a short growing season. Ukrainians brought not only their paska but also their experience in agriculture, which they put to work on thousands of hectares of land in Canada's breadbasket.

The discovery that popular Red Fife wheat could be grown successfully in the province further confirmed Manitoba's position in the grain trade, especially with the invention of the La Croix purifier mill, which turned the flinty kernels of Red Fife into the fine, uniform flour everyone wanted. Commercial mills mushroomed throughout the region, spearheaded by Ogilvie Flour Mills and Lake of the Woods Milling Company. Suddenly, flour became a sophisticated ingredient with names such as Manitoba Patent, Pride of Canada, Manitoba Strong Baker's and Canada's Best. By 1886, exports were booming and production of grain products had become the province's largest economic activity. The milling industry, combined with the arrival of the Canadian Pacific Railway to Manitoba in 1881, made good quality flour accessible to everyone.

Ogilvie Mills
Winnipeg

Bannock

Like bannock, many Manitobans are a melding of Scottish and Indigenous cultures. For generations, Scots from the Orkney Islands came to work for the Hudson's Bay Company in Rupert's Land, often starting families with 'country wives' of Cree or Cree/Scottish origins.

This recipe is from Carol Stankey's grandmother, Margaret Setter Philpott, whose paternal ancestor, Andrew Setter, came from the Orkney island of Rousay in the 1800s to work for the HBC. On January 28, 1821, he married Margaret Spence Batt. She was a descendant of Orkney-born William Sinclair, Chief Factor and Governor at York Factory, and his half-Indigenous wife Margaret "Nahoway," whose grandfather was Cree.

Bannock   Mom
3 C. flour
2 tsp B powder
salt
6 tblsp grease
Warm water
    Make a hole in centre of
mixture, add grease & water.
Sweet as above plus 1 cup sugar
    raisins, 8 tblsp grease

THE SELKIRK SETTLERS COOKED THEIR BANNOCK ON A GRIDDLE, OR AS THEY CALLED IT, A 'GIRDLE' — A FLAT CAST IRON PAN SUSPENDED FROM A SEMICIRCULAR HANDLE — WHICH THEY BROUGHT FROM SCOTLAND.

Tea Biscuits

Tea Biscuits
2 C. flour
4 tsp. b. powder
½ tsp. salt
1½ tblsp shortening
1 C. milk (approx)
  Mix dry content & work in shortening
Add milk so you have a soft
dough that is easily handled.
Roll ¾ inch thick cook at 450° for
          15. min.

A descendant of the Selkirk Settlers, Gordon Cameron remembers his grandmother, Violet White, telling him that her driveway on the farm was so long and so straight, that, when she looked out the window and saw unexpected company arriving, she had time to prepare tea biscuits and have them in the oven by the time her guests walked through the front door.

Ready to prepare the year's first meal of blue geese

Our People, Our Food

Ah, the aroma of roasting goose! Trussed and tied, hanging upside down around the fire, skin sizzling as they spin, slowly turning a golden brown. It's spring and, before the nesting begins, the goose hunt is afoot.

Like the Assiniboine who once lived alongside them, and the Ojibway who came from the Great Lakes to the prairies and the woods, the Plains Cree follow the seasons. The return of the geese signals the running of the sap, as the earth awakens and prepares to share its bounty. It's time to tap the maple and the birch for their sweet juices. The women bring the sap to a boil by lowering fire-heated stones into birch-bark vessels, then stir, stir, stir, until the sweet crystals form.

BERRY PICKING

As the days turn into summer, attention turns to berry picking, the little ones pitching in to help fill the baskets, first with saskatoons, later with blueber-ries and wild plums. A sweet treat, yes, but more than that, a vital ingredient to the sustenance that will carry the community through the harsh winter months.

Pemmican — arguably, the most influential recipe created by the Indigenous peoples of the plains — was quite simply a stroke of genius. A combination of pow-dered bison meat, fat and berries that keeps almost indefinitely, it is packed with protein, vitamins and energy. Best of all, it made use of the most abundant resource on the plains: the bison.

Summer was the time of the bison hunt, when groups of families left the woodlands to follow a herd across

the prairies, the men slaughtering only as many of the
large animals as required for everyone's needs. It
was a busy time for the women and children as well.
Most of the meat was cut into thin strips and dried
on wooden racks, assembled on the spot from branches
transported along with the teepees. If the weather
was sunny, the drying went faster, but clouds or hu-
midity meant keeping a fire going underneath. That was
in addition to the fire for cooking the fresh meat and
rendering the fat for making pemmican.

All this left little time for growing things like
corn, which was available through trade with neighbours
from the south and was planted to a limited extent
throughout the woodlands and prairies. Vegetables and
grains consisted mainly of foraged plants such as sunchokes, prairie turnips and, of course, wild rice.

FALL HARVEST
In the fall, the women harvested wild rice on the
lakes from birchbark canoes. Using the paddles, they
beat the grains into the canoe, every now and then
shaking some into the water to seed the next year's
crop. Every delicious mouthful of the nutty grain we
still enjoy today should come with a dash of thanks
for their gentle wisdom.

Such foresight was not shared by the Europeans who
came to the area, starting in the late 17th century. By
the 1860s, the bison had been brought to the brink of
extinction in the area we now know as Manitoba. While
the Assiniboine had moved on further west, the Cree
and Ojibway remained on the plains surrounding the Red
and Assiniboine rivers, forced to hunt the game that
had originally only supplemented their diet — moose,
rabbit, goose, beaver and deer — along with a variety
of freshwater fish.

Ojibway Tents on Bank of Red River

21

Bread with Potato 'Yeast'

Before the arrival of commercial yeast, many people used a sourdough starter made from potato water, flour and sugar. When commercial yeast finally arrived in Manitoba, it came in the form of expensive cakes. Many people stretched them by adding some sourdough starter. Some bakers even claimed the potatoes gave the bread a silkiness they couldn't get any other way. The Five Roses Cookbook agreed. For this recipe, you can substitute two packets (4½ teaspoons) of yeast.

POTATO YEAST

8 large potatoes
4 tablespoons
    Five Roses flour*
4 tablespoons salt

4 tablespoons granulated
    sugar
4 cups boiling water
4 quarts cold water
2 cakes Royal Yeast*

Peel and boil the potatoes, and mash in water boiled in. Pour this over the flour, salt and sugar (which have been previously stirred together). To this, add boiling water, mix well, then add the cold water. Dissolve the yeast cakes in ½ cup lukewarm water and mix with the above. Let this mixture remain in a warm place about 18 hours. Then it is ready to use. Keep in a cool place and use as required.

BREAD

4 cups potato yeast
1 tablespoon salt
1 tablespoon brown sugar

1 tablespoon butter
8 cups Five Roses flour
    (sifted)*

Set the yeast on the stove and stir until it is at about blood-heat (98F). Then add the salt, sugar and butter. Mix in sufficient flour (previously warmed to room temperature) to make a batter. This will require 3 to 4 cups to the quart of liquid used. Cover and set to rise. When light and frothy, add balance of flour, or enough for dough to cease sticking to the hands. Knead thoroughly for 15 minutes. Let rise again until double original size, when it may be gently moulded into loaves. Let rise again. Then bake 60 minutes in moderate oven.

This recipe calls for Five Roses Flour because it is reproduced from the company's cookbook, but any brand of flour will do. You can also use any brand of yeast.

Driving up to the general store in New Iceland

Every other day, Lara Sigvaldason baked 24 loaves of bread in the wood-burning stove of her home in Arborg. She and her husband, Bjorn, had moved south to Arborg from the Vidir, Manitoba area in 1920, into a house they purchased from the Oblate Fathers, who had used it as an orphanage. Bjorn and Lara raised 16 children in that house, which explains her prolific breadmaking!

Amma Gene's
Icelandic Brown Bread

Kathy Thorsteinson's mother-in-law, Gudny (Gene) Palsson, was renowned for this traditional recipe, shared in the cookbook Arborg & District Multicultural Heritage Village Best Kept Secrets Old and New. In the Palsson household, baking brown bread was a weekly event.

2 cups milk (scalded)
3 teaspoons salt
½ cup brown sugar
3 cups water
5 tablespoons cooking oil

6 cups whole wheat flour
1 cup warm water
2 teaspoons white sugar
2 tablespoons yeast
2 cups molasses
½ – 1 cup white flour

Add milk, salt, brown sugar, 3 cups water and cooking oil to flour and mix. Add warm water, white sugar and yeast and mix. Add molasses and mix. Add white flour (enough white flour so dough doesn't stick) and knead until smooth. Let dough sit for 1 hour, covered. Punch down and let sit for 1½ hours. Punch down again. Separate into six equal portions and work until smooth. Pre-warm six pans and lightly grease. Place dough gently in pans. Bake at 325F for approximately 1 hour.

Sigurdsson & Thorvaldson,
on the east side of Riverton

Amma's Buns

"The little grandkids would sit down for supper and all they would eat was Amma's buns," wrote Barb Orbanski for Best Kept Secrets Old and New. Barb contributed her grandmother Gudrun Johannson's recipe to Arborg's community cookbook. Gudrun was one of 16 children born to Bjorn and Lara Sigvaldason after they moved from Iceland to Manitoba.

Buns (Amma's)

3 cups warm water (I use
2 cups milk (scalded) & 1 water
8 Tblsp. sugar (¼-½ cup)
6 " oil (⅓ cup)
1 tsp. salt
2 Tblsp. Fermapan yeast
2 eggs
7-8 cups flour

Mix yeast in 4 cups of flour.
In separate bowl whip eggs,
sugar, oil & water & milk.
Add flour-yeast mix. Blend
well then grad. add flour.
Let rise 15 min. punch
down. Let rise again for
15 min. Punch down & form
into buns. Let rise for 1 hr.
Bake 350-375 for 15-18 min.

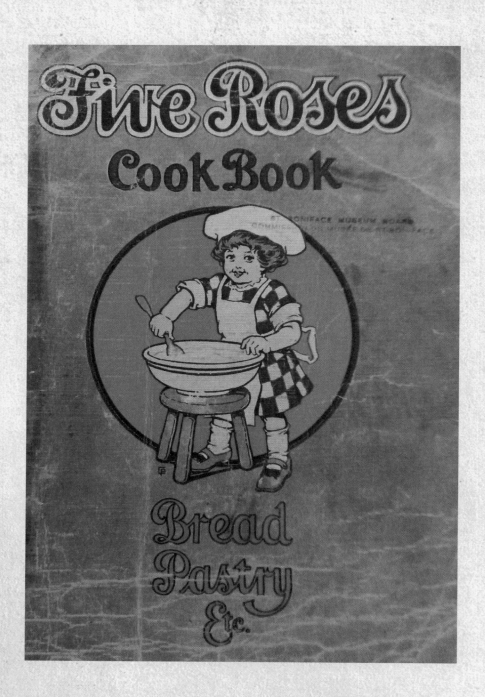

Graham Gems

Popular in the late 19th century, a 'gem' was a type of small muffin made with whole wheat Graham flour. Manitoba home bakers were eager to get their hands on the new 'gem pans' coming up from St. Paul, Minnesota.

Graham flour is named for Sylvester Graham, an early advocate for dietary reform who decried bleaching flour and discarding the bran and wheat germ. Graham flour is more course than whole wheat flour, however, you can use whole wheat flour when making this recipe from the Five Roses Cookbook.

1 cup brown sugar
½ cup lard
1 egg
1 cup sour milk
½ cup Five Roses flour
½ teaspoon baking soda
½ teaspoon salt
½ cup Graham or whole
  wheat flour

How hot was the oven? Before the introduction of temperature gauges, the home baker had a unique way of testing the temperature. She would carefully place her hand in the heart of the wood or coal burning stove and count how long she could hold it there. Comfortable for too long meant more stoking. Pulling out right away meant waiting for the embers to cool. The length of time required to gauge a slow, moderate or quick oven was passed on from mother to daughter.

"Add enough Graham or whole wheat flour to make stiff batter. Bake in buttered gem or muffin tins in quick oven." – Five Roses Cookbook

In olden times, cookbooks often ignored method, oven temperature and time, assuming the home baker would intrinsically know the process, what heat was just right and how long bread, buns, cakes and cookies needed to be in the oven. For these gems, combine brown sugar and lard, beating until smooth. Stir in beaten egg and milk, blending well. Then add dry ingredients, stirring just until combined. You can bake these gems in muffin tins at 400F for 15 minutes.

Popovers

In the late 1800s and early 1900s, recipes had a different format from today's listing of ingredients followed by separate paragraphs for the instructions. Rather, they were often written as one large paragraph with questionable punctuation. This recipe from Mother's Cook Book (1882) is a case in point.

The widespread availability of baking powder at the turn of the 19th century marked a pivotal point in baking cakes and non-yeast quick breads. Its 'double action' meant that the time between mixing and baking was not as critical as with baking soda – previously the only option. The difference is in the production of carbon dioxide, which causes baked goods to rise.

Unlike soda, which releases carbon dioxide all at once when mixed with an acid (such as buttermilk, sour milk, lemon juice or vinegar), baking powder contains two dry acids for an immediate and a delayed reaction. The first rise is activated in the bowl, followed by a second rise activated by the heat of the oven.

In the early days, baking powder was made by pharmacists – known as chemists back then. J.H. Rose, at 302 Main Street in Winnipeg, was one of many local chemists who made their own baking powder. Rose described his product as "pure, strong, healthful; containing only the purest ingredients." At 50¢ a pound – expensive in those days – consumers expected nothing less!

This recipe for popovers promoted use of his baking powder.

For popovers: One pint of sifted flour, one and one-half teaspoonful ROSE's Baking Powder, 1 tablespoon salt, 1 large teaspoonful of melted butter and, lastly, two eggs, beaten very light. Bake in gem or muffin pans.

— ❦ —

Growing up in
New Iceland

Ponnukokur

When Dick Thorsteinson was young, his mother taught him how to make these little pancakes from a recipe passed down from her grandmother, who came from Iceland to live at Bakka, near the mouth of the Icelandic River.

2 eggs
⅓ cup sugar
½ teaspoon vanilla
½ teaspoon cinnamon
¼ teaspoon salt

1½ teaspoons baking soda
½ cup buttermilk
1½ cups flour
1 teaspoon baking powder
2 cups milk

Beat eggs with sugar, vanilla, cinnamon and salt. Dissolve baking soda in a tablespoon of boiling water and add to buttermilk. Add to egg mixture. Gradually add flour and baking powder, beating well. Add milk slowly making sure the mixture is smooth.

   Heat the frying pan to medium. Coat the surface in butter. Pour batter about ¼ cup at a time, spreading until thin. Flip when set. Sprinkle with white or brown sugar and roll. Yum!

Dick's grandfather was an early pioneer in 'refrigeration,' hauling blocks of ice from Lake Winnipeg and placing them, covered with sawdust, inside large semi-buried wooden ice sheds. The ice was used to store fish, the focus of the area's economic activity. Milk and buttermilk were more likely placed in a wooden box and lowered down the well to keep cool. Many homesteads in the area were blessed with good wells providing artesian spring water.

Zwieback.

4. Tassen Milch, oder 4 Tass.
Wasser mit 1½ Tasse Milch-
pulver gemischt.
¼ Tass. Butter
¼ " " Schortning
¼ " " Magarine
¼ " " Oil.

1 Tasse t warmes Wasser
2. Teelöffel Hefe mit 2 Teelöffel
Zucker auflösen.
10 Tassen Mehl.
¼ Tasse Salz in der Milch
auflösen.
      Ofen 425°. 15 Minuten.

"My grandmother Lena made the best Zwieback," says
  Judith Rempel Smucker. Lena Rempel obligingly wrote out
the recipe on a very small scrap of paper in her distinctive
German script. She insisted the secret was in using four
  different kinds of fat: 1/4 cup butter, 1/4 cup oil, 1/4 cup lard
(which she called shortening) and 1/4 cup margarine. In their
many migrations throughout Europe, and eventually to North
  and South America, Mennonites learned to adapt quickly to
new situations and new ingredients. Lena and Jacob Rempel
were among the second wave of Mennonites to come from
Russia to Manitoba. They settled on a farm near Grunthal.

Zwieback

Baked on Saturdays, this double bun with the ball on top is the centrepiece of Sunday Faspa. Before leaving Russia for Canada, Mennonite families filled pillowcases with roasted zwieback, dried for the long journey. Unlike Lena Rempel's recipe, this one uses only two kinds of fat.

2 cups milk
½ cup butter
½ cup lard
2 tablespoons salt
1 teaspoon sugar

½ cup lukewarm water
2 tablespoons active dry
    yeast
4 cups flour (plus up to
    2 more cups in reserve)

Over medium heat warm milk, butter and lard until melted. Add salt. Cool to lukewarm. Meanwhile, stir sugar into lukewarm water, sprinkle yeast and set aside for 10 minutes, until foamed. Combine yeast and milk mixtures.

Gradually mix in 4 cups flour and stir well. Continue adding reserved flour until mixture forms a soft dough. Turn out and knead until smooth and elastic. Let rise until double in bulk, about 2 hours. Punch down and let rise another hour.

Pinch off a ball of dough about the size of a large egg. Place on greased pan and top with a piece of dough the size of a walnut. Space buns 2 inches apart and let rise until double in size. Bake at 400F for 15 to 20 minutes or until nicely browned.

Only the best china would do for Sunday Faspa. Mennonite women treasured their precious plates, cups and saucers carefully wrapped and transported with them from Russia as a reminder of their previous life.

Recipe brought to Canada in 1926
John & Neta Kruger, Brandon, MB

Rollkuchen von Liese.

1. cup whipping cream
1. cup sour cream
¼ cup Milk.
3 Eier.
3 Teeloffel Backpulver
2. Teeloffel Salz.
1. oz. Wodka.

Mehl weich knetten. Morgens ein-
rühren, abends backen. (fridge)
Sour cream erst in die Schüssel + B.pulver
darin auflösen, dann die anderen
Zutaten, dazu tun.

When the Krugers emigrated from the Mennonite
colonies in the former Soviet Union to southern Manitoba
in the 1920s, Neta's sister Lena stayed behind. In the
aftermath of World War II, Lena was banished eastward,
while her sons Hans and John eventually settled in Manitoba.
Neta and John promised Lena they would care for her
children and grandchildren. And they did — including passing
on this traditional recipe that Neta brought with her in
1926 and then re-wrote in a blend of German and English.
Hans' wife Liese passed away in 2001 but Hans continued to
delight in making these rollkuchen well into his 90s.

36

Rollkuchen

A Mennonite summer treat, rollkuchen is traditionally eaten with slices of cold watermelon but it can also be sprinkled with sugar or slathered with jam or honey. This rollkuchen recipe was passed on from John and Neta Kruger to their nephew, Hans Rempel, and his wife Liese.

Mix this dough in the morning to fry it up in the evening.

3 teaspoons baking powder
1 cup sour cream
1 cup whipping cream
¼ cup milk
3 eggs

2 teaspoons salt
1 ounce vodka
Flour to make a soft dough
(about 5 cups)

Stir baking powder into sour cream to dissolve. Add all other ingredients and mix to a soft dough. Store dough in the fridge for about 8 hours or overnight.

Divide the dough into two portions. Roll it out on a floured surface to about ¼-inch thickness. With a sharp knife cut the dough into strips of about 2 inches by 4 inches. Some prefer smaller pieces. Cut two slits down the middle of each piece and fry till golden in deep fat. Lard was traditional, now oil is the norm.

Delisle Bakery on Pembina Highway

Rich Raisin Bread

Variations from the daily bread were a treat enjoyed by settlers across the cultural spectrum. This rasienenstretsel recipe is adapted from Mennonite Foods & Folkways from South Russia, in which author Norma Jost Voth plumbs the pantry of Manitoba Mennonites, among others.

2 cups raisins
2 cups milk
½ cup butter
⅔ cup sugar
1 teaspoon salt
2 packages or 4½ teaspoons
    active dry yeast
2 teaspoons sugar

½ cup lukewarm water
2 eggs, beaten
1 teaspoon grated lemon
    rind
1 teaspoon cinnamon
    (optional)
1 egg
1 teaspoon water
7 – 7½ unbleached flour
    or bread flour

In a small saucepan, cover raisins with water. Bring to a boil, then simmer for 15 minutes or until plumped. Drain and cool.

In a saucepan, warm milk and add butter to melt. Stir in sugar and salt. In a large bowl, sprinkle yeast and sugar over ½ cup water and stir until bubbly. Add milk mixture, eggs, lemon rind and cinnamon, if using. Gradually add half the flour and beat for 5 minutes. Gradually incorporate remaining flour then turn out on floured surface and knead until smooth. Work in raisins.

Cover and set in a warm place until double in bulk. Punch down. Divide dough into three pieces and place in round or loaf pans. Cover and let rise again until doubled. Brush with mixture of 1 egg and 1 teaspoon water. Bake at 350F for 30 minutes.

Our People, Our Food

Lower Fort Garry

When 14-year-old David Thompson arrived at Fort Churchill from England to start his seven-year apprenticeship with the Hudson's Bay Company (HBC) in 1784, he was in for a shock. As a lowly clerk for Governor Samuel Hearne, he was never invited to the mess where the company's officers partook in the European foodstuffs that had accompanied him on the boat. Instead, he subsisted largely on locally-caught whitefish and pike. "We have nothing with them," deplored Thompson, "neither butter nor sauces, and too often not a grain of salt."

The situation didn't get much better when, the following year, he was transferred to York Factory, 200 kilometres southeast of Churchill. By that time, the movement of goods between forts, posts and factories

was well-established, as was the hierarchy of who ate
the best food.

On May 2, 1670, England's King Charles II gave the
Hudson's Bay Company a monopoly over the fur trade in
the land drained by all the rivers and streams flowing
into Hudson Bay. The region was named Rupert's Land
after the company's first Governor, Prince Rupert.
The company was run by the chief factors and traders
but it was the 'tripsmen' who did the heavy lifting
— literally.

FREIGHT CANOE
As such, the story of the fur trade is the story of
food. There was no greater concern than ensuring a
steady flow of sustenance to the tripsmen who plied
the rivers, moving the furs traded by Indigenous
trappers eastward and on to Europe. A northern freight
canoe carried 25 bales of fur and four bags of pemmican. The tripsmen each carried a load weighing 90
pounds. If they were lucky, their provisions included
a bag of hardtack, biscuits made from flour and water,
then twice-baked in the Company's bakehouses. It took
six paddlers an average of 15 days to get to the next
food depot and replenish their allotment of four
daily pounds of food.

Strategic spacing of the food sources led to the
establishment of supply posts such as Lower Fort
Garry, on the Red River north of the Assiniboine,
and Upper Fort Garry, located near the junction of
the two rivers. Eventually, the inhabitants of these
posts planted gardens to supplement their diet while
waiting for the infrequent arrival of supplies — salted
beef, flour, butter, cheese, currants, tea, coffee, rum
— brought thousands of miles from the Old Country.
Jean Drever, later Mrs. W. Cyprian Pinkham, was born at
Lower Fort Garry in 1848. In her memoir Reminiscences
of an Old Timer, she writes of "a great excitement"

when the York boats came, "and the whole village was
on the bank of the river to see them disembark."

Even when Jean's family moved to the Upper Fort,
located near what is now Winnipeg's Broadway and
Main, the menu rarely included fare from abroad. "We
always had plenty of good food. . . my mother made
us children stand around the table while we ate our
breakfast, which usually consisted of bread and milk.
She seemed to think that standing was a healthy way
to take our meals. Pemmican and dried meat entered
largely into our bill of fare." It would be years yet
before the family had cattle and could enjoy beef
roasts, headcheese and sausages.

BISON TONGUE
Meanwhile, back at Lower Fort Garry, Governor Colville
and the officers of the Company were enjoying five meals
a day, including 10-course suppers in the dining room.
Reportedly, bison tongue was the Governor's favourite dish, served, of course, with grainy mustard from
England. Dinners also included bread from the bake-
house located within the stone walls of the fort.
Although the bakers supplied the big house with loaves
and biscuits, their main responsibility was producing
the hardtack that sustained the tripsmen.

As for David Thompson, by the 1850s he had retired
and was living in Upper Canada, his brief career with
the HBC far behind him. It's hard to know whether
it was the bad food or his sense of adventure that,
in 1797 he defected to the North West Company, a
Montreal-based fur trading enterprise in direct competition with the HBC. During his lifetime, he travelled
90,000 km across North America, documenting his ob-
servations, including 20 species of berries native
to Manitoba.

HBC Store in Norway House

HOMESTEADERS SOMETIMES DRIED EGGSHELLS IN THE OVEN,
CRUSHED THEM AND FED THEM BACK TO THE CHICKENS TO
GIVE NEW EGGS A HARDER SHELL.

Paska – Easter Bread

Ukrainians prepare special foods at Easter, including special bread. Joey Stoyanowski remembers his mother, Lena, would always set the dough to rise in the warmth of his second-floor bedroom because it was over the wood-burning stove.

½ cup lukewarm water
2 teaspoons sugar
7 teaspoons yeast
3 cups milk, scalded and
    cooled to warm
3 cups sifted flour
6 eggs, well beaten

1 cup sugar
1 cup butter, melted
Zest of 1 lemon rind and
    1 orange rind
2 tablespoons saffron
1½ teaspoons salt
9 to 10 cups flour
2 cups sultana raisins

Dissolve yeast and sugar in the lukewarm water and set aside for 10 minutes. Put cooled milk into a bowl, add 3 cups flour and beat well. Add dissolved yeast and beat well again until full of bubbles. Set aside to rise in a warm place for 1 hour. This is sponge.

When sponge has risen, add eggs, sugar, butter, zest of rinds, saffron, salt and 9 cups flour. Add from final cup of flour until dough is no longer sticky. Knead until smooth.

Add raisins and knead them well into the dough. Cover and let rise again in a warm place until double in bulk. Shape into round loaves on a greased cookie sheet. Let rise again for 45 minutes in an oven heated to about 100F. Remove from oven.

Heat oven to 350F. Bake for 15 minutes, then reduce heat to 325F and bake another 30 minutes. Remove from oven and glaze with melted butter.

Red River Cereal

Generations of Manitobans started their day with a bowl of Red River Cereal, created in the keystone province in 1924. A blend of cracked wheat, rye and flaxseed, it makes a hearty breakfast. Although not widely available, it can still be found on some store shelves.

1 cup Red River Cereal
4 cups water
¼ teaspoon salt

Combine cereal with water and salt. Bring to a boil, stirring frequently. Reduce heat and boil gently for 5 minutes. Cover and let stand for 5 more minutes. If adding cold milk to the cereal, reduce the cooking water proportionally.

The producers of this iconic cereal named their company and product after the Red River, a well-known symbol of Manitoba. During its history, the province has enjoyed other associations and monikers including 'postage stamp' and 'keystone,' from Governor General Lord Dufferin's description of Manitoba as "the keystone of that mighty arch of sister provinces, which spans the continent from the Atlantic to the Pacific."

St. Luke's Organ Fund
Recipe Book

Winnipeg, Man.
Henderson Brothers, Printers
1910

Soups and Stews

"Soup preceding sumptuous meal, preparing well the way, for happiness and joyous weal, to brighten every day." – St. Luke's Organ Fund Recipe Book (1910)

By 1910, soup had become a starter course for many well-off city folks, but for rural agricultural families, more often than not it was the meal, with its thicker cousin, stew, a worthy upgrade. In the Immigration Halls, built by the government to feed thousands of new Canadians passing through Winnipeg on the way to their homesteads, soups and stews provided a nourishing meal that was easy to prepare in large quantities. Accompanied by a slice of bread or a biscuit, it satisfied the hungry.

Warm comfort

A steaming bowl of meat and vegetables has long been a comforting staple. Every culture has its version of soups and stews. To the first residents of Kildonan, memories of home meant barley floating in a rich mutton broth, while for French Canadian settlers, pea soup was a time-honoured tradition. In their new homeland, Ukrainians continued to enjoy the tart taste of their beet-laced borscht, while Mennonites kept a cabbage version of borscht simmering on their stoves.

From Manitoba's earliest days, its inhabitants were mixing ingredients in a pot. On the banks of the Red River near today's town of Lockport, shards of pottery have been found along with remnants of corn that was added to bison, rabbit, beaver, moose or grouse to make a thick stew.

In his account of a journey from York Factory to Norway House in 1845, HBC tripsman Robert Michael Ballantyne records eating a mixture of pemmican and flour boiled into a sort of thick soup called robbiboo. "It is not a very delicate dish, but is, nevertheless, exceedingly nutritious," he writes, "and those who have lived long in the country, particularly the Canadians, are very fond of it."

Back at Kildonan, the Selkirk Settlers were enjoying Scotch broth, a testament to their perseverance in the farmyard, field and garden. As with most soups, the recipe calls for some basic ingredients, while leaving it open to a variety of options. The thrifty hardworking folks that populated this province knew that the best soups use what you have on hand, including any scraps that need to be used before they spoil.

On the back burner

Soups and stews don't need attention. They can bubble away at the back of the stove on washday and still be ready to fill hungry stomachs when farmers return from the fields.

These one-pot wonders can be celebratory or prosaic, simple or ample. An everyday soup recipe for a family of four can be easily ramped up for a thousand by multiplying the ingredients. It is no wonder that during the Winnipeg General Strike, the Labour League Café was dubbed 'the soup kitchen' by those walking the picket lines.

They weren't the only ones to refer to a meal in this way. "Come have some soup," goes the traditional Franco-Manitoban invitation to supper or 'souper.' More often than not there really was soup on the stove, ready to bring some warmth into a cold Manitoba winter.

Most bison was eaten dried as pemmican, often fried as rowshow (a corruption of the French word 'réchauffe' or warm up) or in a stew variably called 'rababoo' or 'robbiboo.' In the fall, Métis families from St. Norbert and St. Vital brought their livestock south along the Crow Wing Trail (now Highway 59) to the Rat River area near the town of St. Pierre, where there was an abundance of hay. Here, they took the opportunity to hunt bison and make pemmican. Sometimes, if the weather was cold enough during the hunt, they would keep a frozen hindquarter over the winter, either turning it into stew or chipping pieces with a planer. These small pieces, called 'dépouilles,' were fried with onions in a cast iron pan.

Bison Stew

Renowned for using every bit of the bison they hunted, Indigenous people considered certain parts delicacies, such as the hump and the tongue. When, after the Battle of Seven Oaks, Lord Selkirk sent the Des Meurons regiment as military reinforcements to Red River, they were warmly greeted by Chief Peguis and his men. Two dozen warriors prepared a feast of bison tongues for the regiment. For this recipe, bison stew meat will do just fine.

3 tablespoons oil
3½–4 pounds of bison
2 quarts water or beef stock
1 onion, chopped
½ pound mushrooms, quartered or sliced

1 cup carrots, diced
½ cup celery, diced
1 cup turnips or rutabaga, diced
Salt and pepper to taste

Heat the oil in a large pot over medium-high. Brown the meat on all sides. Add water or stock, onion, mushrooms, carrots, celery and turnip. Bring to a boil, then simmer for about 2 hours. Add salt and pepper to taste.

Harvesting root vegetables

Goose Soup

As part of two decades of work on sustainability with 300 First Nations across Canada, the Centre for Indigenous Environmental Resources has collected recipes for food that is hunted, fished or gathered by community people and has been staple to their diet for generations. Maria M'Lot of Manitoba's Cross Lake First Nation contributed this recipe for Goose Soup. "I remember this soup sitting on the back of the stove and people would just help themselves throughout the evening," she wrote in her introduction to the recipe. "This was handy, especially if you were used to having lots of visitors."

1 Canada goose cut into parts
1 onion, diced
2 cups navy beans or another type (rinsed)
Vegetables whatever you have (carrots, celery, potato, turnip, squash, etc.)
Salt and pepper to taste

Cut into parts a plucked, singed and gutted goose with head, wings and feet removed. Place the goose parts and the onion into a large pot of water so that the pot is nearly full. Bring to a boil and add the navy beans. Cover, reduce heat and simmer until the beans are tender. This should take about 4 hours.

While the goose and beans are simmering, prepare the vegetables by cutting them into pieces that are relatively the same size to allow for even cooking time. If you know a vegetable takes longer to cook than the rest you can add it earlier. Boil until all vegetables are tender. Feel free to add salt and pepper as needed or leave as is and people can add their own to their liking.

Serve with bannock and enjoy!

Our People, Our Food

Métis Red River Cart

The peal of church bells announcing midnight Mass is the cue for Julie Riel to open the trap door and fetch tins of tourtières and jars of pickled beets, nestled among the carrots and potatoes in the root cellar of her home at St. Vital, a Francophone community located on the banks of the Red River south of where it meets the Assiniboine. It is Christmas 1869, and there is plenty to celebrate. Her son Louis is at the head of the provisional government, negotiating with Canada for Francophone and Métis rights.

What a spread! In addition to the tourtières (meat pies), there will be boulettes (meatballs), a Métis favourite, and tarte au sucre (sugar pie), a recipe passed down from her Québec-born mother, made with rich cream from the Riel dairy farm.

TRANSFER POINTS

While the HBC men were the first Europeans to work in Manitoba, it was the Francophones affiliated with the North West Company (NWC) who first set down roots and raised their families. Like many of the HBC forts, the

NWC posts such as Fort La Reine and Fort Dauphin to the west, and Fort Rouge near the forks, were transfer points for goods rather than settlements with homes and families. Then in 1806, Louis Riel's grandmother, Marie Anne Gaboury, became the first non-Indigenous woman to set up a household in the region, when she left Quebec to join her husband, Jean-Baptiste Lagimodiere, who was working as a freeman in the fur trade. Not that she lacked company. Marie Anne readily adopted the ways of her Cree and Ojibway neighbours just as the Métis women had done before her.

Who were the Métis? North West Company voyageurs came west from Quebec to work the fur trade, married Indigenous women and, in the process, gave birth to the Métis Nation. Most of the Métis were descendants of the Cree, who were more open to intermarriage than the Ojibway.

The HBC frowned on such local unions, but after retiring from the Company, many English-born HBC men also had families with Indigenous women. The merger of the Hudson's Bay and North West companies in 1821 removed any sense of competition between their Anglophone children and the Francophone Métis. Their cultures blended like the flavours in a good old-fashioned 'rababoo,' the word for stew in Michif, a Métis language that mixes French and Cree with a dash of English.

THE RED RIVER CART

Like their Indigenous ancestors, the early Métis preferred the bison hunt to raising chickens or farming. They were renowned for breeding horses, which they used to pursue the bison on the plains. Groups of families, often numbering in the hundreds, set out together for the hunt. To carry their provisions, they crafted the Red River cart, made only of wood and bison sinew so replacement parts would always be on hand during a breakdown. HBC stores extended credit for supplies, which could include hundreds of butchering knives and dozens of barrels of tea and sugar.

While they searched for the bison herds, they ate
wild game, cooking it over a fire using a tripod and
hook. After the hunt, kettles filled with bison stew
bubbled over the coals while the women pounded dried
strips of bison, combining it with fat and berries to
make pemmican.

By 1835, the Métis had largely supplanted the
French Canadians in the fur trade and replaced the
Indigenous peoples as providers of pemmican for both
the working men and the local population. At the same
time, their horses were avidly sought by HBC officers
eager to engage in sport hunting for various game,
including bison.

Although the fur trade — and the demand for pemmican — started to wane around the mid-19th century, it
would prove too late for the bison. By 1868, they had
been almost exterminated. In fact, so many bison skel-
etons littered the landscape that farmers were willing
to pay up to $6 a ton to have them removed. The Métis
collected them in Red River carts pulled by oxen. The
bones were then sold for making fertilizer and buttons
or for burning into bone char, which was used to
refine sugar.

With the disappearance of the bison, the Métis in-
creasingly turned to agriculture, incorporating more
domestic vegetables and grains into their rich reper-
toire of soups and stews. New varieties of carrots and
potatoes found their way from the field into the cast
iron pot.

MOUNTING TENSIONS

By that time, much of the best farmland had already
been taken by the first and second generations of
English and Scottish settlers. The fact that the Métis
were never granted title to the land on which they
lived created an uncertain future. So, when the government of Canada made a deal with the HBC to offer up
choice parts of Rupert's Land to Anglophone settlers
from Ontario, tensions mounted.

In 1869, the population of Manitoba consisted of

445 Francophone families, 422 of which were Métis. Taken together, the French and English-speaking Métis represented more than 80 percent of the population. Most of them lived on long strips of land extending as much as three kilometres from the rivers. Métis requests to participate in negotiating their own agreement with the government fell on deaf ears. As far as Louis Riel and the Métis were concerned, the arrival of Canadian government surveyors to subdivide their land into square parcels for redistribution to Anglophone Protestant settlers was a call to arms. The events led to the Red River Rebellion, the provisional government led by Louis Riel and, in 1870, the birth of Manitoba as a province.

Métis cottage at Red River

In Kildonan on the Red, Anne Matheson Henderson, a descendant of the Selkirk Settlers, includes a daily menu passed on by her father, Angus Matheson Henderson, a member of the first generation born in the colony. "It was one common in the 1860s," she writes, "but he was of the opinion that menus hadn't changed much from the first days of the settlement, except in quantity and quality." The main meal was eaten at midday rather than in the evening. Most often, it started with a fortifying soup.

BREAKFAST:
Porridge made of cracked wheat or seconds
Bread and milk for the children
Bread or bannock and tea for the adults
Milk, if plentiful, was served on porridge but never any sugar.

DINNER AT MID-DAY:
Generally beef or mutton stock soup with barley and lots of vegetables
Meat or fish and vegetables.
Desserts only on special occasions

SUPPER:
Warmed up potatoes, or some such snack
Bread and butter and tea
Occasionally, as a treat, fresh wild fruit or dried apples

Scotch Broth

Although in Scotland this soup typically used a mutton base, in the early years the Selkirk Settlers often had to settle for broth made from any meat they could get. In 1832, four HBC men made the long trip to Kentucky by horse to buy 1,475 sheep, but only 251 survived the arduous journey back to the colony.

2 pounds of lamb, mutton or beef shanks
8 cups water
½ cup barley (pearl or pot)

1 teaspoon salt
1 onion, 1 turnip, 1 rutabaga and 1 carrot, all chopped

Trim any excess fat from the meat and put in a large pan with the water, pearl barley and salt. Bring to the boil and simmer for an hour.

Add the onion, turnip, rutabaga and carrot. Return to the boil and simmer for another 30 minutes or until the vegetables are just cooked. Remove the shanks from the pot. Trim off the meat and return it to the pot, discarding the bone.

Reputedly, Nellie McClung was horrified by the killing of animals on her family homestead in the Souris River Valley but, although she voiced her disapproval, she still ate meat. Her dumplings on the next page are a perfect accompaniment for beef or chicken stew.

Nonetheless, a life of cooking and cleaning — so called women's work — never appealed to Nellie, even after she married Wesley McClung and went to live above the drugstore he ran in Manitou. Fortunately for us, she eschewed a life of drudgery in favour of helping to form the Women's Christian Temperance Union and later, the Canadian Women's Press Club, from which she emerged as a leader in the local suffrage movement. In 1916, thanks to the group's work, Manitoba became the first Canadian province in which women had the right to vote.

Nellie McClung Dumplings
(for Beef Stew)

For the Selkirk settlers, and later for the Icelandic, Ukrainian and Mennonite pioneers who followed, getting that first cow and steer meant easier access to beef. Every culture had its version of beef stew and dumplings. This dumpling recipe comes from Nellie McClung, a pioneer in her own right. Add these tender morsels of doughy goodness to your favourite beef stew.

2 cups flour
4 teaspoons baking powder
1 teaspoon salt

4 tablespoons lard
⅔ cup whole milk

Mix flour, baking powder and salt in a large bowl. Cut in lard until texture of coarse meal. Add milk and mix. Form into balls about 2 inches across and drop into pot of simmering beef stew. Cover pot and cook stew 15 minutes more.

Newly married and living in Manitou, Manitoba, Nellie McClung was duped into writing a story about her town for the Town & Country magazine by a door-to-door salesman who promised to publish her article if she bought a $5 subscription. Trouble was, the magazine was a fake! Ruefully, Nellie reported that her husband was more enthusiastic when she purchased a $3 cookbook from the next salesman who came to the door.

Bringing produce to town

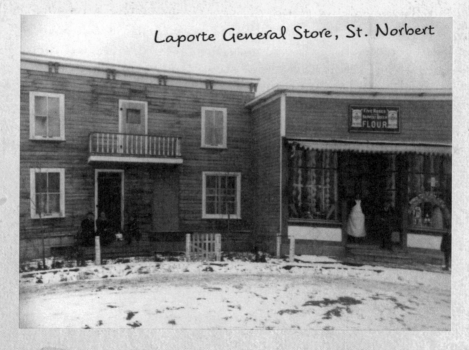

Laporte General Store, St. Norbert

Pea Soup

Lucille Ouimet says yellow peas are essential to this authentic French Canadian recipe. She should know. Her grandparents emigrated from Quebec in the 1880s when Monseigneur Ritchot put out a call for Francophones to populate the land. The couple met in Manitoba and were married in St. Norbert in 1883.

1 pound dried whole
    yellow peas
1 pound of salt pork or
    thick cut bacon, diced
1 medium onion, chopped

2 stalks of celery, chopped
1 teaspoon of salt
¼ teaspoon of pepper
8 cups cold water

Soak peas overnight. Drain and rinse. Place all ingredients in a large pot. Bring to a boil, cover and simmer over low heat for 30 minutes to an hour, or until peas are liquefied, stirring occasionally. If soup becomes too thick, add a bit more water.

I hate it ~ don't make it, Ma!

Pluma Moos

This cold soup was adopted by the Dutch Mennonites when they migrated to Prussia in the 16th century. It proved to be an ideal recipe for those long stretches in Manitoba when fresh fruit and berries were unavailable. It is still enjoyed today.

1 cup prunes
1 cup seedless raisins
¼ cup dried apricots
8 ~~10~~ cups warm water
½ cup sugar

¼ cup flour
½ teaspoon salt
½ cup cold water
1 teaspoon cinnamon

Bring dried fruit and warm water to a boil then simmer until softened. Meanwhile, in a small bowl, make a paste with the sugar, flour, salt and cold water. Add a little of the warm fruit liquid a tablespoonful at a time until paste is runny. Introduce diluted paste into the simmering mixture, stirring constantly. Cook until slightly thickened. Add cinnamon. Cool before serving.

Chicken Noodle Soup

The Mennonite version of this traditional favourite uses star anise as a distinctive flavouring. Some households insist the fully cooked chicken be removed and eaten separately. Others like to leave some of the meat in the soup.

1 stewing hen or
    chicken weighing
    about 3 to 4 pounds
16 cups water
2 teaspoons salt
2 whole star anise

10 whole black
    peppercorns
4 bay leaves
1/3 cup fresh parsley,
    finely chopped
Thin noodles

In a large soup pot, bring water, cut-up chicken and salt to a boil. Simmer for about an hour or until meat falls off the bone. Place spices in a small cloth bag or holder and add to broth. Continue cooking for another 30 minutes. Remove chicken and spice bag from broth. Remove chicken meat from bone and add a generous portion to the soup, reserving the rest for eating separately. Add fresh parsley and your favourite thin noodles. Cook until both are soft.

MaryLou Driedger remembers her grandmother making chicken noodle soup. When people in the Manitoba village of Gnadenthal were sick or going through a difficult time, she would send her son, MaryLou's father, to take them some of the warm concoction. In the winter, he hitched his dog to the sled and delivered the soup that way.

Noodles that are dried for storage will keep indefinitely. In some villages, noodles were given as gifts for Christmas, birthdays and anniversaries.

HOMESTEAD MAGAZINE   NOVEMBER • 17

Home-made Noodles

If you have the time, making fresh rich egg noodles will take your chicken noodle soup to the next level. The ingredients are the same as for kielke (p. 144). The difference is in the preparation. MaryLou's aunts Mary, Margaret and Helen agreed this is the best way to make noodles for soup. Their recommendation: hang them to dry on a laundry drying rack!

3 eggs
3 cups flour
½ teaspoon salt

Enough milk (or water) to
    make firm dough

Break the eggs and mix them with the flour and salt in a bowl.

Move the above mixture to one side of the bowl and add a small amount of milk. Mix in enough flour mixture to begin a dough. Keep adding milk to the flour until all the flour mixture has formed into a FIRM (not sticky) dough. Work the dough with your hands until smooth.

Divide the dough into balls about 4-5 inches in diameter.

Spread flour on a countertop or table and roll out one ball of dough at a time into very thin circles (15-18" in diameter) so that you end up with many flat pieces of thin dough. Keep sprinkling flour on the table and on top of the dough to make rolling easier. The circles should be slightly covered with flour all over. The circles of dough need to dry either on a floured table or hung over a rack. After the dough is dry, place several of the dough circles on top of one another. With a sharp knife cut through all the layers of dough to make about two-inch wide strips. Beginning at the end of a strip, cut dough into very thin noodles. (If the noodles will not be used for soup the same day, scatter the noodles on a floured table for further drying and store in airtight containers for future use.)

69

PROVINCE OF MANITOBA

DEPARTMENT OF AGRICULTURE AND IMMIGRATION

CREAM GRADES

REGULATIONS UNDER SECTION 49A OF "THE DAIRY ACT, 1915" as enacted by Section 4 of Chapter 13, 11 George V.
(Approved by Order-in-Council No. 40001, March 13th, 1923.)
("   "   "   "   No. 41560,   "   10th, 1924.)

The following grade descriptions of cream shall be the only grade descriptions or standards applied or advertised, or otherwise offered or applied in grading cream at any creamery in the Province after the 15th day of March, 1924:

TABLE CREAM

This grade shall include any lot of sweet, clean-flavored, non-frozen cream bought for re-sale for household use. The acidity of this cream shall not be more than twenty one-hundredths (.20%) of one per cent at the time of grading.

This cream shall be produced under conditions that comply with the special requirements of the municipality in which it is to be sold for consumption.

SPECIAL GRADE

This grade shall include any lot of cream which is clean in flavor, of uniform consistency and suitable for making butter of this grade. Its acidity shall not be more than thirty one-hundredths (.30%) of one per cent at the time of being graded at the creamery where it is to be made into butter.

FIRST GRADE

This grade shall include any lot of cream which is reasonably clean in flavor, of uniform consistency and suitable for making butter of this grade. Its acidity shall not be more than sixty one-hundredths (.60%) of one per cent at the time of being graded at the creamery where it is to be made into butter.

SECOND GRADE

This grade shall include any cream that does not meet the requirements specified for the next higher grade; such as cream that is bitter, stale, musty, metallic, or otherwise unclean in flavor.

OFF GRADE

This grade shall include any cream with an objectionable odor or flavor; such as kerosene, gasoline, stinkweed, onions or such other flavors that may render cream unfit for making into number two butter.

SPREAD IN PRICE

A premium of not less than (2) two cents per pound butter-fat shall be paid for Table and Special Cream over Number One, and a premium of not less than (3) three cents per pound butter-fat shall be paid for Number One Cream over Number Two Cream.

The above grade standards and descriptions of cream (amended from those of 1923) are effective from March 15th, 1924, and a copy shall be posted in plain view in the grading room of every creamery operating in Manitoba.

HON. A. PREFONTAINE
Minister of Agriculture and Immigration

L. A. GIBSON
Dairy Commissioner

Butta Zupp

Despite the name, this potato-based soup hardly contains any butter at all. There is "just a little blob added at the end to enrich the soup, which is generally made without meat," notes Doris Penner, a food writer for Steinbach's newspaper, The Carillon. This recipe is adapted from her files.

BUTTA ZUPP

2 quarts water
6 potatoes, peeled and cubed
1 medium onion,
    coarsely chopped
2 bay leaves
3 tablespoons fresh parsley,
    chopped (or 2 teaspoons dried)
A few peppercorns
1 cup noodles
1 tablespoon butter
½ cup cream (half and half)

Add water, potatoes, onion, bay leaves, parsley and peppercorns to a large soup pot. Bring to boil, then cook on medium heat until vegetables are done. Return to boil and add noodles (store-bought or homemade as for chicken noodle soup), stirring to separate. Just before serving, add butter and cream to soup. Makes 5 or 6 servings.

In 1900, butter traded or sold for nine cents a pound. World War I drove the price up to 60 cents, the same price as a dozen eggs.

UKRAINIAN-ENGLISH COOK BOOK

УКРАЇНСЬКО - АНГЛІЙСЬКА КУХАРКА

Часть II.
СТАРОКРАЄВА
ДОМАШНА
КУХНЯ

72

Borscht

Mary Wyporowich left Ukraine in 1902 as a one-year-old and came to Poplarfield, where she later met her husband, Andrew Klowak, who came from Ukraine at the age of 12 in 1906. Their youngest daughter, Sandra, grew up watching her mother make traditional Ukrainian dishes in their homestead kitchen. Today, Sandra has her own favourite recipe for borscht, which calls for the addition of cream just before serving. Some prefer adding sour cream into each individual bowl. Either way, this soup is delicious!

Borsct (Beet soup)
4 med. size beets, shredded - (boil separately)
10 cup water
1 qt. beef broth
1 onion chopped - 1 tbsp salt - 1 bay leaf
3 carrots cubed - 2 potatoes shredded
3 stalks celery chopped
½ cabbage shredded
Boil beets till almost tender.
In a large pot — water, broth, seasoning,
vegetables, bring to boil, cook about 45 min.
Add beets, boil at least ½ hour together
When tender, add 1 cup peas & chopped dill.
Season to taste. Add ½ cup whipping cream
mixed with flour & some beet soup to cream borscht.

Komst Borscht

This Mennonite adaptation of the well-known Ukrainian soup does not use beets, but is heavy on the cabbage (komst) instead.

2 pounds beef soup bones
12 cups cold water
4 cups cabbage, chopped
1 carrot, sliced
1 large onion, chopped
1 small bunch each
   parsley and dill,
   chopped

1 bay leaf
Salt and pepper to taste
4 cups tomatoes, roughly
   chopped
Heavy or sour cream
   (optional)

Boil soup bones in water for 1 hour. Add cabbage, carrot, onion and herbs. Season to taste with salt and pepper. Boil for another hour. Adjust seasoning if necessary. Add chopped tomatoes and boil for another hour. Serve with heavy or sour cream, as desired.

Zumma Borscht

After a long winter, Mennonite homesteaders were eager to harvest the fresh sorrel that gives this summer (zumma) soup its tangy taste. This recipe is adapted from the Mennonite Cookbook compiled by the Altona Women's Institute.

8 cups boiling water
½ pound smoked ham or
   sausage, cubed
1 tablespoon salt
4 cups potatoes, cubed
2 cups sorrel (or beet tops),
   chopped

1 cup green onion tops,
   chopped
¼ cup fresh dill, chopped
1 tablespoon fresh
   parsley, chopped
1 bay leaf
½ cup heavy cream

In a large pot or stockpot, bring water to boil and add smoked pork or sausage. Remove from heat and let cool 30 minutes. Add salt and potatoes, bring to a boil and cook for 5 to 10 minutes. Add sorrel or beet greens, green onions, dill, parsley and bay leaf, and cook for 20 to 30 minutes or until vegetables are tender. Just before serving, remove from heat and add cream.

Flesh, Fish and Fowl

"No hunter shall hunt, trap, take or shoot at, wound or kill any bison or buffalo at any time." — Western Farmers' Handbook (1910)

When the first fur trade posts were built on Hudson Bay, wild game was scarce in the area. The men of the post depended on fish as a local source of sustenance, along with the twice-yearly delivery of salt pork and beef from England. In his diaries, explorer and HBC man David Thompson explained that every time a new trading house was opened, the men were anxious to know the quality of the fish in the adjacent lakes and rivers. In the winter, they often lived on fish for months on end.

Frozen fish

"A fish, once frozen, loses its good taste unless kept in that state until it is thrown into a kettle of boiling water," writes Thompson. Even so, without salt, fish was bland. On the other hand, all the meat that came on the boat from England was too salty and had to be soaked in the lake for days before it was boiled. When the HBC realized they could employ Indigenous people to hunt geese, grouse, ptarmigan, deer, beavers, caribou and rabbits, meals improved exponentially.

The voyageurs of the North West Company (NWC) were much quicker to adopt the food habits of their Indigenous brethren. Pemmican became a main-stay of their diet. Once the HBC caught on, supply of the high-energy mixture of suet, berries and bison could barely keep up with demand. Meanwhile, back at the fur depots such as Lower Fort Garry, the supply of meat was sporadic. In the 1850s, Governor Colville's Métis cook, Johnny Garten, knew how to make rancid meat palatable with a dash of

Worcestershire sauce, imported from England.

As for the Selkirk Settlers, initially their only source of fresh meat was wild game, mostly ducks, geese, prairie chickens, wild turkeys and rabbits, which were dried and stored for the winter. Eventually cattle, sheep and chickens augmented the daily diet, not only with a wider variety of fresh meat, but also with cured bacon, ham and blood pudding.

However, despite the importation of livestock by the settlers, Manitoba's game stocks became seriously strained. "By the mid-1850s," wrote Alexander Ross, a NWC trader who later became the first sheriff in the Selkirk Colony, "the wild animals of the chase had almost ceased to exist there, in sufficient numbers, at least, to feed and clothe the aboriginal inhabitants of the soil – not that such number had been extirpated by the natives themselves, but by the destroying hand of civilized man."

Spring floods

During the recurrent spring floods, the colony loaded their livestock on York boats and moved up to Lake Winnipeg where they lived primarily on fish. The lake provided for the Selkirk settlers as it had always done for the Indigenous people who were there before them, and as it would for subsequent newcomers to this harsh land.

For the first few years after their arrival, the Icelandic settlers also survived by their catch, eating fish morning, noon and night, breakfast, lunch and dinner, broiled, stuffed and brined. Only the Mennonites and Ukrainians avoided this fate, avidly breeding the pigs and cows with which they made the kielbasa and farmer's sausage that have become staples of the Manitoba diet.

PLAINS CREE FAMILY - WESTERN MANITOBA CIRCA 1900

Beaver Tail and Moose Nose

These traditional recipes come from Ruth Christie, an Elder from Peguis First Nation, born in Loon Straits on Lake Winnipeg. She is the granddaughter of John Ramsay, who was a member of the Sandy Bar Band, a group of Cree and Ojibway people.

Beaver tail

Broil the tail over hot coals for a few minutes. The rough, scaly hide will blister and come off, leaving the tail clean, white and solid. Then roast or boil until tender. This is considered very strengthening food. Use only young beaver.

Moose nose

Impale the cut end of the nose on a sharp stick. Singe off the heavy dark hair thoroughly after turning it over a steady fire. Soak overnight in salted water. Brush with a wire brush the next day to remove all burnt residue. Cut into large pieces to expose the inner sinus cavities. Singe again to remove this hair too. Wash in salt water and brush with wire brush until clean. Boil the pieces with an onion, vinegar and peppercorns for approximately 6 hours, adding water to keep it covered. Remove and reassemble pieces into nose shape and place on platter. Cool. The juices will jell to aspic.

In her memoir, Reminiscences of an Old Timer, Jean Drever recalls attending parties near Upper Fort Garry in the 1860s where she was served "a very good supper, consisting of bison and deer tongues, beautifully corned, moose nose and beaver tails."

A good day's catch!

Sturgeon in Wine Sauce

Manitoba's Indigenous peoples used elaborate weirs to catch sturgeon, which they ate fresh, smoked and dried. The meaty fish was also a favourite in the Governor's dining room at Lower Fort Garry, where this recipe originates.

1 tablespoon butter
1 cup white wine
1 cup milk
½ teaspoon each, salt and pepper

2½ pounds sturgeon or other firm white fish such as halibut or cod, cut in 6 pieces
2 tablespoons green onions, finely chopped
¼ cup parsley, finely chopped

Melt butter in a large frying pan. Add wine and milk. Cook for 2 minutes on medium heat until milk curdles. Strain through a fine sieve. Return to heat and bring to a boil, adding salt and pepper. Poach sturgeon in liquid 10 to 15 minutes, depending on thickness of pieces. Remove from pan onto warm platter. Add green onions to liquid and continue cooking until reduced to half. Pour over fish. Sprinkle with chopped parsley.

Once plentiful in Manitoba's lakes and rivers, sturgeon was also a source of isinglass, a substance made from the swimming bladder and used by early settlers to thicken jellies and blancmange before gelatin became readily available.

Corned Beef

Refrigeration was a challenge that could be met only partially by iceboxes and root cellars. Meat was often salted, brined, smoked or corned for preservation. The term 'corned' is derived from an old English word for large coarse grains of salt used to cure the meat. This recipe comes from Phyllis Fraser, a descendant of the Selkirk Settlers.

For 5 or 6 pounds of beef brisket, make brine of:

Enough water to cover the meat by 1 inch
7 tablespoons salt

3 tablespoons brown sugar
2 tablespoons saltpetre

Place uncut meat in a large container with a lid. Measure out the amount of water needed to cover the meat. Transfer water into a large saucepan and add the rest of the ingredients. Boil liquid, cool and pour over the meat. Let stand 5 or 6 days in the refrigerator, turning meat once each day, then boil beef gently in the brine, 3 or more hours until fork tender.

In the days before refrigeration, farm families joined cooperative beef rings. During the summer, a steer was killed each week and the beef distributed among members of the ring. Families took turns providing the steer and receiving each type of cut. In the winter, beef rings were unnecessary because meat could be frozen and stored for long periods.

Tourtière

Originally made with game such as venison, this traditional French Canadian dish evolved as game was replaced with livestock. This recipe, which uses ground pork and beef, comes from Lucille Ouimet, whose Quebec-born grandmother might well have occasionally used wild game when she made tourtière in St. Norbert.

Tourtières - Meat Pie
5 lbs meat 2½ Pork lean & 2½ lean Beef.
3 medium onions minced through grinder
4½ ts salt
1½ ts sage
1½ ts dry mustard
½ ts cloves
1½ cup potato water
3 large potatoes cooked & mashed without adding anything in the potatoes
Allow to cook for 20 minutes, then add the mashed potatoes, mix together & let it cool
Make about 10 medium or 5 large meatpie

Pork Hocks

Franco-Manitobans were steadfast Catholics, observing all the religious holidays. Throughout Advent, approximately four weeks preceding Christmas, they abstained from eating meat on Wednesdays and Fridays. At the same time, they prepared for the révéllion, the feast that followed midnight mass on December 24, by cooking traditional meat dishes such as tourtières, boulettes and pork hocks. This recipe for pork hocks is adapted from Culinary Heritage Gems of St. Norbert Pioneer Families.

2–4 meaty pork hocks
1 onion, finely chopped
1 large bay leaf

Salt and pepper to taste
¼ cup flour
2 tablespoons water

Place hocks in a heavy pan and roast for 15 minutes in a 350F oven. Drain and reserve fat, transferring a few tablespoons to a large pot. Heat fat and just before it smokes, add pork to brown on all sides. Cover hocks with hot water. Add onions, bay leaf, salt and pepper. Simmer 2 to 3 hours or until meat is tender and falls off the bone. Cool enough to handle then remove hocks, reserving the meat and discarding the skin and bones.

Chill and skim fat from broth. (Reserve the fat and some of the broth for other recipes, such as Boulettes.)

Spread flour in a heavy saucepan and cook in 350°F oven until browned (about 10 minutes, with a quick stir half-way through). Remove from oven and add water to make a thin paste. Bring hock broth to a boil and add gradually to flour paste, stirring constantly to avoid lumps. When gravy has thickened, add meat from hocks to reheat. Do not boil. Adjust seasoning.

Traditionally served with boiled or mashed potatoes, cabbage salad and pickled beets.

New Year's
Feast at the
home of
John Monias

Boulettes (Meatballs)

Métis culinary traditions focus on simple hearty adaptations of Indigenous and French-Canadian foods. Some versions of this recipe add carrots and potatoes. Others stick to the meatballs. This should make enough for six people.

8 cups water
Salt and pepper to taste
6 medium potatoes
    peeled and cut in
    quarters (optional)

6 medium carrots cut in
    pieces (optional)
2 pounds of ground beef,
    moose or deer
3 large onions, diced
Flour

In a large pot bring water to a boil, adding salt and pepper, along with potatoes and carrots, if using. Mix ground meat and onions, form into 2-inch balls and roll in flour. Drop meatballs gently in boiling water, then lower heat and simmer for 1 hour. Mix 2 tablespoons of flour with 2 tablespoons of water in a small bowl. Add 4 tablespoons of cooking liquid and stir until dissolved. Add contents of small bowl to pot and stir until thickened.

In 1873, members of the Sandy Bar Band were relocated from their community on the shore of Lake Winnipeg to make way for the Icelandic settlers. One of those who lost his home was John Ramsay. Despite the loss, he reached out to the newcomers and helped them survive through the first difficult years. He took time to teach them how to ice fish with a jigger, hunt for moose and smoke fish to preserve it.

In the winter of 1876, a smallpox epidemic decimated both the Indigenous and Icelandic communities near the Whitemud River. John Ramsay lost his sons and his wife, Betsey. Four years later, he marked her grave with a marble headstone purchased from Lower Fort Garry and built a fence around it. Legend has it that in 1908, settler Trausti Vigfusson repaired the fence after a request from John Ramsay, who appeared to him in a dream.

Suckers

Every spring, Ruth Christie could hardly wait for her father to take her fishing for suckers. When the ice flows started to come in from Lake Winnipeg, they would take the canoe to a swampy area at the edge of the lake near Loon Straits and portage to the creek that spilled into the lake. As the suckers came over the waterfall, she scooped dozens of them into her net. "They taste just like salmon," she says. There were always enough to eat some fresh and also to pickle a bunch for later.

1 quart sealer, cleaned and rinsed with boiling water	4 tablespoons oil
	5 tablespoons crushed tomatoes
1 large sucker	1 tablespoon pickling salt
4 tablespoons vinegar	

Cut fish into pieces, put into sealer. Add vinegar, oil, tomatoes and pickling salt. Process 4 or 5 hours until tight seal is formed. Store in a cool dark place.

In home canning terms, 'processing' means submerging sealed jars in a large pot of cold water that is then brought and kept at a low boil. This destroys microorganisms that cause food to spoil and vents excess air from the jar. Venting causes air pressure outside the jar to be greater than inside so the lid is pushed down for a true vacuum seal.

Royal
Alexandra
Hotel

Royal
Alexandra
Hotel kitchen

Goldeye

With a coppery exterior and tender pink flesh tinged
with red at the edges, goldeye – or tullibee – is smoked
whole. A favoured treat in New Iceland, this local
delicacy spread far and wide after the railway reached
Gimli in 1906. It was introduced to Winnipeg at the
CPR's Royal Alexandra Hotel, then made its way
from the dining cars of the CPR to Chicago's and New
York's finest hotels. In 1919, goldeye from Manitoba
was served to King George VI and U.S. President
Woodrow Wilson at the Grand Café in New York.
Today, it is arguably one of Manitoba's signature foods.

Here is a simple recipe for those who want to try
their hand at smoking this delicate fish.

Enough goldeye to fit
   into a 3-gallon pail
16 cups water

½ cup pickling salt
1 cup brown sugar

Pack fish tightly into a 3-gallon bowl or pail. In
a large pot, heat water on low. Add salt and sugar
stirring until dissolved. Pour brine over fish and leave
in a cool place overnight.

Rinse off brine and lay fish out on a tray to dry
for at least 30 minutes. Smoke with willow or oak
for 3 to 3½ hours or until flesh is firm and opaque,
and skin takes on a golden red hue.

Raising sheep near Riverton

Rúllupylsa

Before coming to Manitoba, Icelanders raised sheep in their former homeland. The fatter, less desirable cuts were pounded thin, rolled and brined for a delicacy called Rúllupylsa. It was a few years before the settlers could import sheep to New Iceland to make this beloved treat, served thinly sliced on brown bread. It is still available at some stores in the Interlake.

2 pounds lamb flank
1 tablespoon onion, chopped
2 teaspoons salt

½ teaspoon pepper
½ teaspoon ginger

FOR BRINE:
4 quarts water (16 cups)
½ teaspoon saltpetre

1 cup salt
¼ cup brown sugar

FOR COOKING:
Water to cover
3 whole cloves

¼ teaspoon allspice

Flatten the lamb flank with a mallet. Sprinkle with onion and spices. Roll tightly and secure with string in all directions. It is important that the roll remains as tight as possible.

Place brine ingredients in a saucepan and boil for 5 minutes. Cool before pouring over lamb. Refrigerate for one week, turning roll every two days.

Remove from brine. Place several spoons at the bottom of a large saucepan and gently lower roll over this 'stand.' Cover with water. Add cloves and allspice. Bring to a boil, then simmer for 3½ to 4 hours. Drain carefully, allow to cool, then 'press' overnight with a heavy object such as a wrapped brick. Pat dry of any remaining liquid. Serve cold.

Winter fishing camp
in New Iceland

Baked Stuffed Whitefish

In 1877, whitefish was plentiful in Manitoba. At a rate of 3 ½ to 4 cents a fish, it was also hard work. Fishermen traveled great distances and often had to overnight at fish camps far from home. Fortunately, they almost always brought back some of their catch to feed their families. The Icelandic settlers enjoyed the delicate flesh, especially stuffed and baked. The key is not to overcook it.

1 whole whitefish
2 slices day old bread
1 medium onion, chopped
½ cup celery, chopped
½ teaspoon of salt

Dash of pepper
½ teaspoon each thyme, marjoram and sage
½ cup butter, melted
1 egg

Wipe dry the inside of the gutted fish. Tear bread into small crumbs and combine with all other ingredients in a bowl. Stuff bread mixture into the cavity of the fish. Bind fish with twine and sprinkle with salt and pepper. Place in an oiled ovenproof pan and bake at 400F for 10 minutes.

The commercial fishermen of New Iceland plied their trade on Lake Winnipeg, Lake Manitoba, Winnipegosis and anywhere else the catch was good. In the winter, they transported their catch from the fish stations to buyers in Gimli by dog or horse-drawn sleds — later by bombardier, a large enclosed wooden snowmobile. In the summer, boats like the Keenora and Lady of the Lake made the rounds between fish stations and the processing plants in Gimli, Selkirk and Winnipeg.

Fish boxes pulled by dog sled on Lake Winnipeg

Pan-fried Pickerel

As whitefish waned in popularity, it was replaced by pickerel, aka walleye, on Winnipeg plates. With its light taste and delicate flesh, it continues to enjoy widespread popularity.

¼ cup flour
¼ teaspoon salt
¼ teaspoon pepper

2 pound pickerel fillets
3 tablespoons butter
4 lemon wedges

Combine flour, salt and pepper in a shallow dish. Lightly coat both side of each fillet in flour mixture. In a skillet, heat butter until bubbling, then fry fish a scant 2 minutes per side. Adjust time according to thickness.

Lake Winnipeg

Fried Pickerel Cheeks

Despite being less well known, these fleshy fish cheeks are a prized delicacy.

2 pounds of pickerel
   cheeks, rinsed
Salt
1 cup flour

1 cup fine breadcrumbs
2 eggs, lightly whisked
Oil

Pat the cheeks dry and lightly season with salt. Place flour, breadcrumbs and eggs, each in a separate bowl. Coat the fish first in flour, then eggs and lastly breadcrumbs.

   Heat about ½ inch of oil in a pan until just about to smoke. Lower heat to medium. In batches, fry coated fish pieces until golden brown, turning halfway. Remove and drain on paper. Salt to taste.

Pig farming in Manitoba

Jreeve and Rebspäa

In the fall, three or four Mennonite families convened for a killing bee to slaughter the hogs they had fattened all summer. A few days before the event, all utensils and crocks were scrubbed clean. On the day of the bee, the men sharpened their knives before dawn as they waited for the women to finish preparing breakfast.

After breakfast, the men killed the animals and started a fire under a large kettle or 'miagrope' to boil water for scalding the carcasses. Nothing went to waste. As a pig was butchered and portioned into chops and roasts, pieces of pork fat and meat scraps were ground up and cooked in another miagrope, reserved for rendering. As the cracklings were reduced to crispy nuggets, a couple of ribs or 'rebspäa' were tossed in to cook.

Purely delicious

"The purely delicious smell of roasting pork mingling with a faint overlay of wood smoke was one of the benefits of standing at the miagrope and stirring the mixture," recalls Marlene Plett in her autobiography An Unhurried Journey: The Road from Edenthal. "It was fascinating to watch the women, skilled and fearless, test the doneness of the cracklings by running an index finger through the hot, bubbling lard. If it was a good heat, but not scalding, it was time to extract the spare ribs, lard and cracklings from this massive pot."

When the bones could be loosened with a twist, the ribs were ready to be fished out with a long-handled meat fork exclusively used for this purpose. The cracklings were ladled out and passed through a sieve to drain off the clear lard, which was poured into crocks and stored for use in baking.

After a long hard day, these succulent ribs or 'rebspäa' were especially delicious. The cracklings or 'jreeve' were saved for the next morning, to be spread on warm slices of fresh baked bread. Leftovers were packed with a thick layer of lard, stored for another breakfast or for sprinkling on fried potatoes.

Our People, Our Food

Warm fresh bread slathered in butter. Is there a more delicious treat? Better still, Mrs. Robert Henderson tells William Healy, author of Women of Red River, spread it with browned flour and molasses right after it comes out of the outdoor bake oven. But not even that could taste as good as the first bite of bread taken by her grandmother, Anne Bannerman, a full six years after leaving Scotland to settle in the harsh land along the Red River.

In 1811, Thomas Douglas, the Earl of Selkirk, was given authority over 300,000 square kilometres of land along the banks of the Red River by the Hudson's Bay Company. His goal was to help resettle 270 Highlanders, evicted from their homes by Scottish landowners who favoured sheep ranching.

SURPLUS PRODUCE

The Company was keen on the idea of the Selkirk Settlers cultivating the land. "All the surplus produce such as flour, beef, pork and butter, articles the Company requires, would by means of the colony be obtained more conveniently, cheaper and with less risk, than by annual importation of such articles from England," reports Alexander Ross in his book Red River Settlement, written in 1856. Accordingly, each Selkirk Settler was given 100 acres (40 hectares) of land at five shillings per acre, payable in produce.

But they were given little else. In fact, they would
not have survived the first year without the help of
Chief Peguis and the Indigenous people from the Netley
Creek area, just north of the Selkirk settlement.
Travelling from Fort York on Hudson Bay down to the
Forks of the Red River and the Assiniboine, the settlers arrived in October, too late for planting. They
would have starved had not Peguis and his band shared
their food and showed the Scots how to hunt for game,
forage for roots and berries, and fish for pike, sturgeon and walleye. For a while, wild turnips replaced
'neeps' in the Scottish diet.

"I can remember hearing the old people when I
was in my childhood, speaking of the Indian remedy
for scurvy, which was a drink made from the sap of
the white spruce," another descendant of the Selkirk
Settlers told Healey many years later.

When winter arrived, the settlers were again saved
from starvation by their Indigenous neighbours, who
walked them 112 kilometres south to Pembina where
food was more abundant. Later, Peguis was officially
recognized by Lord Selkirk as a friend of the settlers.

On the other hand, the North West Company and
the Métis did not welcome the rise of the Red River
Settlement. Instead, they saw it as a move by the
HBC to gain more control over trade in the region.
Subsequent events would prove them right. In the mean-
time, the Selkirk Settlers contended with grasshopper
plagues and flooding that forced them to take refuge on
higher ground. Under the circumstances, food became a
constant concern.

PEMMICAN PROCLAMATION
On the pretext of ensuring adequate supplies for
the settlers, the Governor of Assiniboia, Miles
Macdonell, issued the infamous Pemmican Proclamation
on January 8, 1814:

"Whereby, it is hereby ordered, that no person
trading furs or provisions within the territory for

the Honourable Hudson's Bay Company, or the North West Company, or any individual or unconnected trades or persons whatever, shall take any provisions, either of flesh, fish, grain, or vegetable, procured or raised within the said territory, by water or land carriage..."

To the NWC and the Métis who provided pemmican for voyageurs going west, this was a thinly veiled ploy to stop the trade that was so necessary to their livelihoods. In retribution, they raided and burned down the settlers' homes and their bastion, Fort Douglas. The HBC retaliated, burning several NWC posts, including Fort Gibraltar at the Forks.

Tensions came to a head on June 19, 1816, at the Battle of Seven Oaks. A group of NWC-affiliated Métis and their leader, Cuthbert Grant, raided HBC's Brandon House to reclaim a supply of pemmican the HBC had earlier taken from the Métis. They planned to sell it to the NWC at a meeting place just north of the Red River Settlement. On the way there, they ran into the new HBC governor, Robert Semple, and his men at an area known as "La Grenouillère" or Frog Plain, not far from a stand of seven oak trees. In the ensuing battle, 21 men were killed including Semple and several settlers.

TURNIPS AND WHEAT

Undaunted, the settlers rebuilt their homes, planted new gardens — including 'neeps' or turnips — and even tried planting wheat in the area they affectionately named Kildonan, after the Scottish valley where most of them were born. The first variety of wheat, English white, was very susceptible to frost. When the women and children joined the men to hasten the harvest, no one was left in the kitchen to make the round unleavened loaves, called bannocks. After the harvest, everyone helped to replenish the flour bin by grinding the wheat with querns, their traditional handmills brought over from Scotland.

Gradually hardier varieties of wheat were introduced, along with windmills to make it easier to grind the grain. In 1823, 300 head of cattle were brought in by American traders, followed by another importation of steers and milk cows two years later. Roast beef and cheese found their way onto the tables of Kildonan for the first time in 10 years. It was a welcome change from the stinky cheese purchased at the HBC store, or the salted beef that had to be soaked in plenty of water before it could be tossed in a stew. By the 1840s, as supplies started to come up the trail from St Paul, Minnesota, by Red River cart, an even greater variety of food became available, along with cookware, utensils, stoves and fuel.

Red River Settlement House in Kildonan

St. Boniface Butcher

Cretons

In the late 1880s, as pork became more available, Franco-Manitobans rediscovered the art of making cretons, a breakfast staple of their Québécois ancestors. In Manitoba, they are eaten more as a snack than as part of a meal, spread on toast much like Mennonite cracklings.

1½ pounds ground pork with a high fat content

1 onion, finely chopped

2-3 cloves of garlic, minced

1 cup breadcrumbs

1 cup milk

1 pinch each ground cloves, cinnamon

Salt and pepper to taste

Place first four ingredients in a saucepan. Stir in the milk. Add seasoning. Cook on low heat for about an hour, stirring occasionally, until most of the moisture has been absorbed. Cool completely before serving.

House in
East Reserve

Farmers' Sausage

Farmers' sausage is perhaps the most popular – certainly the most ubiquitous – Mennonite food enjoyed by Manitobans. During hog killing bees, women cleaned the intestines for use as sausage casings by passing knitting needles through them as scrapers to remove fat and tissue. Then they turned the intestines inside out, washing and scrubbing them three or four times with hot water, bran and salt. Lean meat trimmed from the bones, the ham and front shoulders was ground, seasoned with salt and pepper, and stuffed into the casings. The sausages were then smoked for several hours before being buried in the wheat bin, which became a natural freezer in the winter.

Lafrance & Barrette
BOUCHERS

Ancienne place Lauzon, Bonnick, McCormick & Cie., au Coin de l'Avenue Taché et de la Rue Dumoulin.

Headcheese

Headcheese has deep roots in Manitoba, from the Scottish settlers to the Mennonites, from Franco-Manitobans to Ukrainians. Despite its unsavoury name, it was a popular way of using the 'extra bits' of beef or pork that had not been made into roasts, hams, blood puddings or sausages. Mennonites eat this pork version sliced with vinegar.

1 part pork rind, cleaned and cooked

2 parts pork meat, cooked
Salt and pepper

Put rind and meat through the meat grinder. Add salt and pepper to taste. Place in a loaf pan with the liquid stock from the cooked meat. Cool. Cover with a solution of 2 parts water and 1 part vinegar. Keep in a cool place for three to four days. Slice and serve with an extra sprinkling of vinegar, if you wish.

Throughout their history, Mennonites endured repeated episodes of forced migration, first within Europe and then to North and South America. Faced with frequent hardship and deprivation, they focussed on simple hearty fare in which not a scrap of food is wasted.

Growing corn in New Iceland

The
Earth's Bounty

"Potatoes are in the best condition for use in late summer and autumn." – Blue Ribbon Cook Book, Winnipeg edition (1905)

In early spring, when fresh vegetables were scarce and shelves in the root cellar were almost bare, Annabelle Gunn, born in the Red River Settlement in 1872, foraged for lamb's quarters to use as a potherb. Known on the prairies as pigweed or fat hen, the entire plant is edible when steamed and eaten like spinach. Along with wild leeks, dandelions and tender shoots of nettle, they were the first greens of spring to land in Annabelle's kitchen.

'Three sisters'

Before Europeans came with their carrots and cabbages, their wheat and barley, the prairie soil provided for its people with native plants such as sunchokes, mushrooms and wild rice. Along with foraging, the Cree and Ojibway also carried out some limited cultivation of corn, beans and squash, the so-called "three sisters." Evidence of this activity was uncovered in the area known today as Lockport, as well as at the forks of the Red and Assiniboine Rivers.

These traditional Indigenous foods were an important source of nutrition for the first settlers. As soon as they could, the Selkirk settlers and, later, the Icelandic immigrants sent for seed from Europe to cultivate the familiar vegetables and grains of their homelands. Ukrainian homesteaders brought seeds with them, sewed into the lining of the clothes they wore on their trip overseas. Some varietals grew in Manitoba and some faltered, so the reliance on native cultivars never entirely disappeared. Instead, the newcomers adapted their recipes and their cooking.

In the heart of a prairie winter, everyone was reduced to eating turnips, parsnips, cabbage, potatoes and carrots, longing for the tender greens that came with spring.

„Ярини"

Cooking under a wigwam frame

Wild Rice

The Ojibway called it manomin, which means 'gift from the Creator.' Wild rice is a European misnomer, as this nutty-flavoured grain is not a rice at all, but a cereal grass that grows exclusively in water. After harvesting, the grains were spread on long woven mats stretched across a scaffold built several feet over a smouldering fire. This parching of the grains dried the manomin for preservation and also opened the hulls for threshing off the chaff, which was done in large bark trays.

1 cup wild rice
3 ½ cups water

1 teaspoon salt

Rinse the wild rice. Drain, then add to a heavy saucepan along with water and salt. Bring to a boil. Reduce heat to simmer and cook, covered, 40 to 50 minutes. For chewer texture cook less time. Drain any excess liquid.

Substituting water with chicken or beef broth will add even more flavour. To reduce cooking time, soak wild rice overnight. Be careful not to overcook. When grains puff open, manomin is ready to eat.

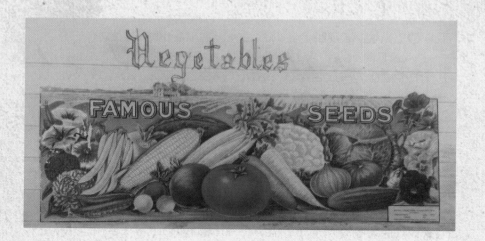

Clapshot

Many of Manitoba's Indigenous people have dual heritage — tracing their lineage through both North America and Europe. Both cultures have had a strong influence on what goes on in kitchens across the province. Ruth Christie is a case in point, tracing her heritage to the shores of Lake Winnipeg and to the Orkney Islands of Scotland. This recipe harkens back to Ruth's Scottish roots.

Clapshot (a dish from the Orkney Islands)
1 lb of potatoes, peeled
1 lb turnips
2-4 tbsp drippings
2 tbsp chives, chopped
salt and pepper
Cook and mash potatoes, cook and mash turnips. Beat the vegetables together. Stir in drippings to taste, then check the mixture for seasoning. Beat the clapshot over heat until well mixed, then serve piping hot.

IN W.J. HEALY'S BOOK WOMEN OF RED RIVER, ELIZABETH, THE WIFE OF MANITOBA PREMIER JOHN NORQUAY, WHO SERVED FROM 1878 TO 1888, TELLS THE AUTHOR THAT, WHEN FOOD WAS SCARCE IN THE EARLY YEARS, THE SELKIRK SETTLERS LEARNED FROM THEIR INDIGENOUS NEIGHBOURS TO FORAGE FOR WILD TURNIP, KNOWN AS 'ASKIPAWAH.'

Lamb's Quarters

Pick the plant when it is young and tender. Flash cook like spinach in a few tablespoons of water. Sprinkle with salt and a few drops of vinegar before serving.

Wild Leeks

Wash and parboil the entire plant for 5 to 10 minutes. Finish by frying in butter. Because garden leeks are substantially larger than the wild variety, if using, slice into ¼-inch pieces before frying.

Chickweed

Use only in early spring, before flower heads start to form. These tender plants can be added to other salad greens and finished with a simple oil and vinegar dressing, along with grated cheese and tomatoes.

Dandelion Salad

Today, many Manitobans think of dandelions as weeds, but to the first homesteaders they were the season's first salad greens. For this tasty recipe, pick the plants before the flower buds form.

   Use leaves and white stalk above the root. Be sure to wash thoroughly.

   Cook bacon and reserve fat. Allow fat to cool but not solidify. Mix with an equal amount of warm vinegar. Add crumpled bacon and pour over dandelion greens just before serving. If you make the dressing in advance, keep it slightly warm until ready to use.

Joyal family garden in St. Norbert

Our People, Our Food

Imagine serving supper for 35 — then doing it all
again for a second sitting! That doesn't take into
account the children who eat in the kitchen while
the adults enjoy wine with their meal in the dining
room. The tables are laden with roast pork, chicken
and veal, as well as countless tourtières. Desserts
abound, from doughnuts and tartes au sucre to fruit
pies and baked apples with cream. Such is New Year's
Day at the Bohémier house in 1904.

OFFICIALLY BILINGUAL

Benjamin Bohémier and his wife Marie-Louise Limoges
migrated from Quebec to St. Norbert in 1883, among
the many Francophones encouraged by Archbishop Taché
of St. Boniface to start a farm in the west. When
Manitoba entered Confederation in 1870, the province
was officially bilingual. Over the next 20 years, thousands of French speakers from Quebec and New England
heeded the call, including two Bohémier families.

The clergy encouraged the newcomers to settle
together and foster FrancoCanadian culture in communities such as Sainte Agathe, Lorette, Saint Adolphe
and many more. These communities preserved a distinct
culinary tradition, replete with pea soup, fèves aux
lards (baked beans) and tourtière, along with sweet
crèpes, taffy and sucre à la crème (fudge).

These everyday eats and special treats had a place
at the Bohémier family table 20 years later. By that
time their sons and daughters had started their own
households. Now numbering close to 60, the close-knit
family still gathered at the original Maison Bohémier
on special occasions.

Like the Métis before them, the francophone settlers had large families. Both groups also had very
close ties to the church. Back in 1818, the Roman
Catholic Church had sent Father Provencher to the Forks
of the Red and Assiniboine rivers where he founded the
diocese of St. Boniface and later became its Bishop.
Provencher's main goal was to bring the Indigenous
and Métis into the Catholic fold and, to that end,
he brought from Quebec the Grey Nuns and Oblates as

teachers, along with a number of families. A testimony to his success is the Métis' strong devotion to the Catholic faith, echoed by the Francophones who subsequently settled St. Norbert and the rural communities.

Unlike the Métis, who had a long tradition of fishing in places such as St. Laurent on Lake Manitoba, this new wave of settlers was more interested in raising cattle and pigs than casting nets. They rarely ate fish, except on Fridays as mandated by the church. Even then, it was more likely to be salted than fresh-caught.

Nonetheless, the cultural and culinary overlap was significant, with language the main ingredient in a strong bond. Hoping to build up from this base, francophone community leaders convinced French-speaking immigrants from Europe to establish parishes such as Notre Dame de Lourdes. But this last effort to reverse the ongoing Anglicization of Manitoba was to no avail.

Although their numbers had grown, the province's Francophone community could not keep pace with the influx of newcomers from Ontario and Europe. By the mid-1890s, French speakers in Manitoba represented less than 10 percent of the population.

Laporte General Store, St. Norbert

Dried Beans and Peas

Baked Beans

Like many homemakers of her generation, Josephine Grégoire Bonhémier wrote and pasted recipes in her notebook, including this one for traditional French Canadian baked binnes from Sister St. Jacques in Lorette. Josephine's grandmother came to Manitoba from Quebec in the late 1800s.

5 cups dry white beans
½ cup molasses or brown
   sugar

1 tablespoon mustard
1 small onion
5 strips thick-cut bacon

Cover beans with an inch of water and soak overnight. Drain. In a pot, cover beans with water and bring to a boil. Simmer for 30 minutes. Drain. Combine with other ingredients in an ovenproof dish.

Cook at 350F at least 3 hours or at 300F for 5 to 8 hours.

"Now that the family is smaller," wrote Josephine in her notebook. "I only cook 2 cups beans in my little crockery pot."

Sam Dong, c. 1920

Weekes Studio

128

Chop Suey

In the 1880s, Chinese men who had built the railway to Canada's west coast came to Manitoba looking for work. Some settled in Winnipeg while others were drawn to the city of Brandon and its surrounding towns and villages. Many opened restaurants, introducing prairie diners to new tastes and foods, such as soya sauce and rice. They also adapted recipes to local ingredients and palates with dishes such as this chop suey.

2 cloves garlic, minced
2 tablespoons soy sauce
2 tablespoons water
1½ teaspoons cornstarch
1 pound lean pork,
    cut in strips
2 ribs celery, diagonally
    cut into ¼-inch long
    pieces
¼ pound mushrooms,
    sliced thick

1 onion, halved
    lengthwise and into
    ¼-inch-thick strips
1 green pepper, cut into
    ¼-inch-thick strips
1 small Chinese cabbage
    (suey choy), cut into
    ¼-inch-thick strips
2 tablespoons oil
1 teaspoon cornstarch
¼ cup chicken broth

Stir together garlic cloves, 2 tablespoons soy sauce and ½ teaspoon cornstarch in a bowl. Stir in pork and marinate 15 minutes.

Keep each vegetable separate. Heat a frying pan or wok over high heat until a bead of water dropped onto cooking surface evaporates immediately. Drizzle 1 tablespoon vegetable oil around side of pan, then stir-fry celery, until crisp-tender, about 2 minutes. Transfer celery to a large bowl. Reheat wok and stir-fry each remaining vegetable separately in the same manner.

Drizzle second tablespoon of oil in hot pan. Cook pork until no longer pink. Return vegetables to pan and toss with pork. Combine broth and cornstarch in a small bowl. Make a well in center, then stir broth mixture and add to well. Bring sauce to a boil, undisturbed, then stir to combine with pork and vegetables. Serve immediately, with cooked rice.

Scalloped Cabbage

Cabbage grows well in Manitoba. Sometimes home-steaders were victims of their own success. As the heads kept rolling in, new recipe ideas were always welcome. Winnipeg's Blue Ribbon Company was only too happy to oblige and promote its products in the process. Here is a prime example:

Cut boiled cabbage in pieces; put in buttered baking dish, sprinkle with salt and Blue Ribbon pepper, then add medium white sauce. Lift cabbage with fork that it may be well mixed with sauce. Cover with buttered bread crumbs, and bake until crumbs are brown.

MEDIUM (WHITE) SAUCE:

2 tablespoons butter   1 cup milk
2 tablespoons flour   ½ teaspoon salt.

Melt butter in a saucepan. Add flour to form a paste. Add milk, a little at a time, being careful not to form lumps. Stir constantly over medium low heat until thickened.

THE BLUE RIBBON COOK BOOK LISTS THREE CATEGORIES OF WHITE SAUCE — THIN, MEDIUM AND THICK. THE ONLY DIFFERENCE IS THE AMOUNT OF FLOUR AND BUTTER, FROM 1 TABLESPOON OF EACH FOR THIN UP TO THREE TABLESPOONS FOR THICK.

О. ЗАКЛИНСЬКА

НОВА КУХНЯ

ВІТАМІНОВА

В-во. РУСАЛКА

Kutya

Mary Marcinkow is devoted to preserving her Ukrainian heritage. Every Christmas Eve, she prepares the kutya, one of the required 12 dishes at the celebration. In Mary's home, after the head of the family imparts the Christmas blessing, everyone partakes in kutya — but only a spoonful, to leave room for the 11 other traditional dishes that follow.

1 cup wheat kernels with or without bran
4 cups water
½ cup poppy seeds

½ cup honey (Mary says buckwheat honey is the best)
½ cup boiling water
½ cup walnuts or pecans, finely chopped

If using wheat kernels with bran, toast in slow oven until warm to the touch, then sprinkle with water. Place in a sturdy cloth bag and pound with a rolling pin until bran is released.

Soak naked kernels in 4 cups water overnight. Drain, reserving liquid. Simmer in soaking water for 4 to 6 hours until tender, adding more water if necessary. Meanwhile cover poppy seeds in warm water and soak for 30 minutes. Drain well then grind to a fine texture.

Add honey, poppy seeds and ½ cup boiling water to cooked wheat, stirring gently. Sprinkle with chopped nuts.

It is traditional to throw a tablespoon of kutya at the ceiling. If it sticks, it is a sure sign that you will have peace and prosperity in the year to come.

Bubble and Squeak

In the last quarter of the 19th century, the arrival of a large wave of Anglo-Ontario migrants prompted the appearance of traditional English dishes in Manitoba cookbooks and kitchens. This recipe for using leftover vegetables gets its name from the sound the cabbage makes in the pan.

3 tablespoons butter
1 onion, sliced
2 cups cooked cabbage
   or any mixture
   of leftover cooked
   vegetables

2 cups leftover mashed
   potatoes
Salt and pepper to taste

Melt 1 tablespoon of butter in a frying pan. Cook onion over medium heat until softened. In a large bowl, combine cooked onions with cabbage or vegetables, potatoes and seasonings. Melt remaining butter and turn vegetable mixture into the pan, pressing until it starts to squeak. Cook until bottom starts to crisp then invert onto a plate and serve.

Latkes

The first wave of Jewish immigrants arrived in Manitoba from Russia in 1881, introducing Winnipeggers to these tender little potato pancakes. Over the years, successive waves of Jewish immigrants joined the first 33 families, many settling in the city's North End.

4 – 5 large potatoes, grated
½ cup onion, finely grated

2 eggs
¼ cup flour
1 teaspoon salt
¾ cup oil

Place grated potato and onion in a colander and press out excess water. Combine in a bowl with eggs, flour and salt. Heat oil in frying pan. Drop by tablespoonful into hot fat, turning to brown both sides. Remove and drain excess oil on paper before serving.

Bakka house on the Icelandic River, pre 1910

Manitoba Mainstays

"Everybody had a summer kitchen. When you didn't cook in the house, it was cool when you went to sleep at night." – Sandra (Klowak) Rychliki

Today, Manitobans can buy ready-made perogies, cabbage rolls, tourtière and kielke (egg noodles) at the grocery store, thanks in large part to the immigrant women who spent hours over their hot stoves keeping these traditions alive, while keeping their families fed. The heat generated from preparing these culture-defining dishes was more than welcome on cold winter nights, but not so much during the sweltering days of summer.

Summer kitchen

Fortunately, most homes had a summer kitchen. From the time of the first Selkirk Settlers, French-Canadians and Métis to the Ukrainians, Poles and Mennonites, a cooking area separate from the house was seen as a must to keep the living and sleeping quarters comfortable.

Many settlers and homesteaders built the summer kitchen as a separate structure to reduce the risk of fire. However, since this meant carrying pots of food a greater distance from stove to table, some preferred to attach the second kitchen to the exterior of the house.

That was the case in the Riel family home. Unfortunately, a chimney fire started in the summer kitchen and the entire house went up in flames. It was rebuilt by Joseph, Louis Riel's brother, who nonetheless refused to change the design. In wintertime, the stove was moved back into the house and the attached, uninsulated summer kitchen served as convenient cold storage for food and firewood.

Sandra Rychliki recalls how, over the winter, her mother, Mary Klowak, stored barrels of sauerkraut in the summer kitchen, which was a separate building on her family's homestead. Both the main house and the summer kitchen had their own stoves. Like their neighbours, the Klowaks also had a root cellar filled with beets, carrots and lots and lots of potatoes. "When the new crops came in, the potatoes in the root cellar were still firm," she says. That meant perogies could be filled with potatoes all year round – or sauerkraut for that matter, as both fillings were favourites.

The ice box

Keeping food cold in winter was no problem but summer was another story. Starting in the mid-19th century, the icebox gradually became a mainstay of Manitoba kitchens. In the winter, ice haulers cut and delivered large blocks of ice a metre square for storage in each family's ice house, a shed often built half underground. Covered in sawdust, the ice remained solid for much of the summer. Pieces were chiseled off and inserted in the top of the insulated icebox to cool the contents below. Those who didn't have an ice house received more frequent deliveries of ice, in blocks the size of the icebox. As the ice melted, sometimes the small pieces were used in the ice cream maker to churn out a Sunday treat!

Perogies

Ukrainians refer to their popular dumplings as pyrohy, often misheard by anglophones as 'pedaheh.' Most of us know them by their Slavic or Polish name 'perogy.' Sandra Rychliki grew up watching her Ukrainian mother make perogies and carried on the tradition. This is her favourite recipe for the dough.

Perogy Dough
3 cups flour
1 tsp salt
1 1/4 warm water
1/4 . cup oil
Mix all together – knead on counter
till dough is smooth (2 or 3 min)
Let dough rest before rolling (about 1 hour)
Fill as desired. Boil: put into boiling
water, boil 3 min. after water comes to a
rolling boil. Drain, add butter & serve.

Sandra claims that the secret to a good potato perogy filling is the right cheese. Some cooks like to use cottage cheese but she prefers the tangy taste of cheddar.

In 1896, Manitoba had 52 cheese factories, precursors to Bothwell Cheese, founded by Frank Giesbrecht and Bernhard Dueck in New Bothwell 40 years later — and still in business today.

POTATO AND CHEESE FILLING

1 tablespoon onion, grated
2 tablespoons butter
2 cups cold mashed
   potatoes

2 cups good quality
   cheddar, grated
Salt and pepper

Cook the onion in butter until tender but not brown. In a large bowl, combine it with the potatoes and cheese. Season to taste with salt and pepper.

Roll the dough thinly on a floured board. Cut rounds with a large cookie cutter or the open end of a glass. Place a spoonful of filling on each round and fold over into a half circle, pressing firmly closed.

Drop perogies gently into a large pot of boiling water and cook until they rise to the top. Serve plain or with fried onions and sour cream.

Ukrainian thatched buildings near Fraserwood

Vereniki

Is it a perogy or a vereniki? After living for generations in Russia, it's not surprising that Mennonites adopted and adapted their neighbour's favourite dishes, and then brought them to Manitoba. Their version of the Ukrainian perogy, differentiated by the Mennonite name 'vereniki,' is filled with cottage cheese and served in a delicious cream sauce.

DOUGH

¼ cup milk
¼ cup light cream
2 egg whites

1½ cups flour
¼ teaspoon salt

Mix milk, cream and egg whites. In a separate bowl, combine flour and salt. Make a well in the centre and add milk mixture, stirring until combined into a pliable dough. Gather into a ball and let rest for an hour.

FILLING

2 cups dry cottage cheese
2 egg yolks

Salt and pepper to taste

Mix ingredients in a bowl. Roll dough on a well-floured surface to about ¼ inch thickness. Cut into 3-inch squares. Place a spoonful of filling on each square. Fold over and pinch closed. Boil 12 cups water with 1 teaspoon salt and 1 tablespoon oil. Place pockets gently in boiling water, about 10 at a time. Cook until they float to the top. Scoop from the water, drain and cook the remaining pockets. Serve with cream sauce.

CREAM SAUCE

2 tablespoons butter	¼ teaspoon salt
½ cup heavy cream	

Melt butter. Add cream and salt. Bring to a boil and cook until slightly thickened. Be careful not to over-cook. If mixture becomes too thick, add more cream.

Life on the farm

Kielke

Mennonites picked up a passion for noodles during their time in Prussia and made them their own. These delicious tender ribbons were enjoyed at many-a-Manitoba table after young Mennonite women from the East and West Reserves left their communities to work as housekeepers in Winnipeg. Today, locally-produced kielke can often be found alongside Italian pasta at the grocery store. Made fresh, they are even more delicious. This recipe is adapted from Neubergthal's Centennial cookbook.

5 eggs
⅔ cup water

2 teaspoons salt
5 to 7 cups flour

Mix ingredients and knead until smooth, adding only enough flour until the dough is not sticky. Roll into a rectangle about ¼-inch thick. Cut into 1½-inch wide strips and then cut across the strips to make ¼-inch wide kielke. Drop into 12 cups boiling salted water. Cook 5 minutes and serve with schmaunt fat, fried onions, fried sausage or ham.

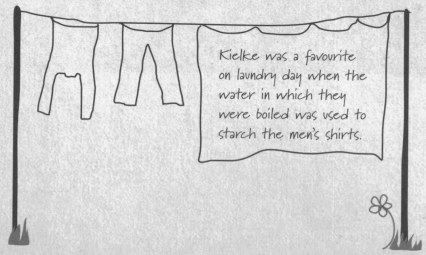

Kielke was a favourite on laundry day when the water in which they were boiled was used to starch the men's shirts.

Schmaunt Faht

Norma Giesbrecht says kielke is best when made with a stiff dough, then boiled and served with plenty of fried onions or, even better, fried the next day until crispy. When she serves it fresh, she makes schmaunt faht sauce with a little bit of cream. Some prefer to use a lot.

To make schmaunt faht, start with hot drippings from ham or sausages in a small saucepan on medium heat. Brown half a tablespoon of flour if using ¼ cup cream, or two tablespoons of flour if using a whole cup. Lower heat and add cream gradually, stirring until thickened. Take off heat and pour over kielke.

Although she now lives in Altona, Norma grew up in Neubergthal where her grandfather, Bernardt Hamm, built a typical Mennonite home with the barn attached. With a cow always within reach, there was never a shortage of cream for the gravy!

Carrying cream to the railway station at Malonton

IN THE EARLY 1890S, MANITOBA SAW THE ARRIVAL OF THE COOLEY MILK CAN, WITH A GLASS PANEL ON THE SIDE. THANKS TO THIS FEATURE, IT WAS EASY TO SEE HOW MUCH CREAM HAD RISEN TO THE TOP. THE ADVENT OF THE CREAM SEPARATOR IN 1900 MADE LIFE EVEN EASIER!

Delivery time

Holubtsi (Cabbage Rolls)

Literally translated, the Ukrainian name for these stuffed cabbage leaves means 'little pigeons.' For Christmas Eve, Ukrainians make a meatless version and use buckwheat instead of rice.

1 large head cabbage
2 cups rice
2 cups boiling water
2 teaspoons salt
1 medium onion, finely
   chopped

4 to 5 tablespoons butter
1 cup crisp bacon,
   chopped
1½ cups tomato juice

Core the cabbage and place it in a deep pot. Pour boiling water into the hollow core until the head is completely covered. Let it stand until the leaves are soft and pliable and the water has cooled. Drain the cabbage and carefully peel off the leaves without tearing. With a sharp knife, carefully shave down the centre rib of each leaf to create a more pliable envelope. Line the bottom of a large shallow ovenproof dish with any broken leaves.

For the filling, rinse rice then add to salted boiling water and let cook 1 minute. Remove from heat, cover, and let stand until all the water is absorbed. Meanwhile, cook the onion in butter until softened. Mix onion and cooked bacon with the partially-cooked rice.

Place a generous spoonful of filling on a cabbage leaf and roll up, tucking in the ends. Place rolls in casserole dish and sprinkle with salt and pepper. Continue adding in layers. Pour tomato juice over the rolls. Bake, covered, at 350F for 1½ to 2 hours, until both cabbage and filling are cooked.

Pyrizhky

In Ukrainian 'pyr' means banquet and that is often where these little buns are served today. No wonder Sandra Rychlicki's recipe makes 14 dozen!

1 cup lard
½ teaspoon salt
4 teaspoons sugar
4 cups flour
½ cup warm water

1 teaspoon sugar
2¼ teaspoons yeast
1 cup sour cream
3 eggs, well beaten

In a large bowl, cut lard into mixture of salt, 3 teaspoons sugar and flour until consistency of oatmeal. Dissolve 1 teaspoon of sugar into warm water and sprinkle yeast on top. Let sit 10 minutes until foamy then add to flour mixture. Stir in sour cream and eggs, mixing well with a wooden spoon. Cover bowl and let dough rise in a cool place for 3 hours.

Roll dough ¼-inch thick. Cut dough into 2-inch squares. Fill with preferred filling and press closed into little oblongs. Bake on greased cookie sheet at 325F for 20 minutes or until golden brown. Brush with melted butter.

Sauerkraut is the most popular filling, although onion, cottage cheese and mushroom are options as well.

SAUERKRAUT FILLING:
1½ to 2 quarts sauerkraut
1 large onion, finely
    chopped

4 to 5 tablespoons oil
½ cup fresh dill, chopped

Rinse sauerkraut, squeeze dry and chop fine. Fry onion in oil over medium heat until tender but not brown. Add onion and dill to chopped sauerkraut and bake in oven at 300F for about 45 minutes, stirring every 15 minutes. Cool before filling pyrizhky.

Ukrainian women
picking cabbages

Homesteaders from Germany often
shared their sauerkraut cutters with
their neighbours. Shredded cabbage
was packed in crocks between layers
of salt then covered and weighed
down with a stone until fermented,
about four to six weeks.

Our People, Our Food

New Iceland

It must have been the aroma of baking bread that drew
them. In a single day, the home that Jodis 'Disa'
Brandson shared with her husband Siggi (Sigruidur)
and their 10 children in New Iceland received no less
than 40 visitors. They were all welcomed with a cup
of coffee and a slice of bread. Good thing she liked
to bake!

In fact, Disa enjoyed baking so much that rarely a
day passed without her hands in flour, bread rising near
the stove. On another fateful day, company showed up
on route to Winnipeg. After visiting for a while, they
invited the Brandsons to join them on their outing.
But what about the bread that was still proofing, Disa
wanted to know. The only solution was to bring it along
and bake it in the city. The bread rose so high in the
hot car that they had to stop in Teulon and punch it
down before they could keep going.

It had not always been so easy to travel the 100
kilometres between New Iceland and Winnipeg. In fact,

when the first 250 Icelandic settlers arrived in October
1875, they made the journey by boat. With the ice
forming on Lake Winnipeg, they were unable to proceed
further up the Red River than a creek south of what
would later become the town of Gimli, or 'heaven'
in Icelandic. They were forced to unload their food,
cooking utensils, seeds and materials for nets, and
build 30 temporary cabins to overwinter.

A NEW LAND
Driven from their homeland by volcanic eruptions
and failing crops, the Icelanders had made a failed
attempt at relocation in Kinmount, Ontario, before
Immigration Agent John Taylor and Governor General
Lord Dufferin made it possible for them to settle in
a tract of land 10 kilometres wide and 58 kilometres north of Boundary Creek on the west shores of
Lake Winnipeg.

By the late summer of 1876, joined by 1,100 more
settlers, they had built farmhouses, imported livestock
and started fishing operations. The Indigenous population shared with the newcomers their techniques for a
successful catch both summer and winter, underpinning
what would soon become a vibrant commercial fishing
enterprise.

Before long, fathers and sons, uncles and nephews
were setting out over water or ice to commercial
fishing camps across the lake. At the end of the season,
they brought some of the whitefish back to their families for cooking, stuffing, pickling and salting.

Meanwhile, with the men away, mothers and daughters tended the cows and chickens that produced milk
and eggs for yoghurt-like skyr and ponnukokur pancakes.
Just like in Iceland, they made brown bread because
molasses cost less than sugar.

With the arrival of the railway in the late 1870s,
demand for whitefish and pickerel (aka walleye) grew
beyond the borders of New Iceland. As the fishing industry continued to expand, so did the number of

lumber mills providing wood for the boxes used to transport the fish. Business boomed among those who cut large ice blocks from the lake to keep the catch cold. Eventually a fish plant was built. Steamers from the fish processing plants came by the camps once a week to pick up the fish and drop off supplies.

In the 1870s, the province of Manitoba was tiny, extending approximately 200 km east to west and 175 km north to south — aptly named the "postage stamp" province. Located outside the provincial boundaries, New Iceland was a temporary 'republic' with its own constitution, until Manitoba's borders were expanded in 1881. The Icelandic settlers eventually spread out as well, beyond the original communities such as Gimli, Riverton, Hnausa and Hecla to homestead in the area between lakes Winnipeg and Manitoba — known as the Interlake — especially along the Icelandic River.

While it's now rare to see whitefish on the menu, the delicate taste of pickerel continues to be popular in Manitoba kitchens.

Convoy of fishing boats on Lake Winnipeg

Notes

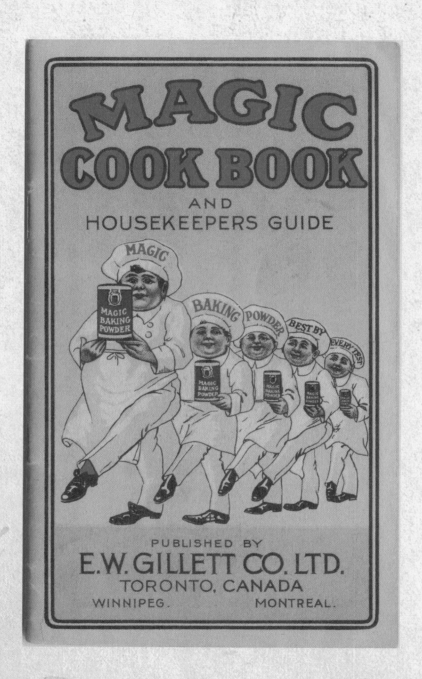

MAGIC COOK BOOK

AND
HOUSEKEEPERS GUIDE

PUBLISHED BY

E.W. GILLETT CO. LTD.
TORONTO, CANADA
WINNIPEG.   MONTREAL.

Cakes and Sweet Treats

"They set special store by the currants that we always put in the round cakes which we gave them at New Year's with tea." – Mrs. Inkster, resident of Kildonan in the 1860s, writing about the annual delivery of cakes to her Indigenous neighbours.

What is a celebration without a cake? Sunday afternoon tea without cookies? In the early years, sugar was scarce and making sweets was a rare event. The first source of sugar came in the form of large bricks, from which portions were chipped off with a chisel. No wonder many preferred to use molasses, which was also more readily available. Eventually, pantries with two pull-out bins became a household fixture, one holding 100 pounds of flour and the other 100 pounds of sugar, purchased twice a year from the grocery store.

Stoves arrive

The act of baking became easier as well. Hearths were replaced with stoves that burned wood, then coal, kerosene oil, gas and eventually, electricity. Early recipe books gave advice to cooks and bakers on how to adjust for the best results. Using a wood stove? Don't disturb the fire while baking to ensure an even heat. Cooking with kerosene? Don't overfill the pans in case they overflow into the flame.

Baking powder opened up so many possibilities – but only if you were careful. The Winnipeg version of the Magic Cook Book and Housekeepers Guide, published in the 1920s, warns of door-to-door canvassers flogging fake baking powder. Spiked with albumen to make it froth when added to cold water during the sales pitch, this fraudulent substitute was in reality a far inferior product.

The fact that these modernities coincided with the advent of the threshing machine placed a new emphasis on preparing a superior dessert. Since few farmers could afford this expensive implement, most of them depended on traveling threshing crews, some better than others. Crews gravitated to those farms that provided the best food, and a creative cake was the ultimate measure of success. The competition became so heated that it generated discussion in the Grain Growers Guide, published weekly between 1908 and 1928 by the United Farmers of Manitoba. This missive from 'A Happy Farmer's Wife' appeared in Letters to the Editor on April 20, 1910: "I get what I know will be quite sufficient bread baked and in the cellar a day or two before I expect them; also make stacks of pies and fruit cakes, also vanilla, almond and sponge cakes, which will only take a few minutes to ice when wanted."

The importance of cake

Meanwhile, cakes continued to be a hallmark of entertaining. From oat cakes to matrimonial cake, platz to vinarterta, molasses cookies to peppernuts, home baking was key to receiving visitors, whether you were a Mennonite mother preparing for Faspa or a member of the province's business elite hosting the ladies of the Winnipeg Musical Club. "I have a bunch coming here tomorrow for tea and music so spent this morning baking cake and cookies," wrote Irene Evans in 1915 to her husband William Sanford Evans, onetime mayor of Winnipeg, while he was away on business. For rich and poor, rural and urban, recent immigrant and long-time resident alike, sweets held a special place at any event.

Chocolate Chiffon Cake

This recipe comes from the diary of Neil Van Dusen's grandmother, Agnes Matheson, born in the Red River Colony in 1856. Agnes was a descendant of Alexander Matheson, one of the original Selkirk Settlers. The recipe has been passed down for more than four generations.

Chocolate Chiffon Cake

Cake part - 1 cup hot water, ½ cup Cocoa, ⅞ cups flour (all purpose) 2 tsp. baking powder, ¼ tsp soda, ½ tsp salt 1 cup white sugar (fine) ¼ cup corn oil, 3 egg yolks ½ teaspoon vanilla 3 egg whites ¼ tsp cream tartar.

Combine hot water & Cocoa, Boil 1 minute stirring constantly, Cool.

Sift flour, baking powder, soda, salt and sugar into a bowl - Add cooled cocoa syrup, Corn oil, vanilla & egg yolks - blend smoothly -

Beat egg whites with Cream of tartar, until very stiff - Fold egg whites into first mixture blending carefully -

Bake in ungreased 8 inch tube pan in moderate oven 350 F. for about 45 minutes

Suspend like angel Cake till Completely Cool

Frost when Cool with orange icing -

Icing -

Two table spoons butter
¼ tsp lemon extract
½ tsp grated orange rind
2 cups sifted icing sugar
3 table spoons orange juice
Beat till smooth & creamy
Decorate with melted bitter chocolate

Oat Cakes

In 1813, a second batch of Selkirk Settlers landed on the shores of Hudson Bay, where they were forced to overwinter before making the 965-kilometre trek south to Red River the following spring. Among them were families named Sutherland, Matheson, Gunn and McKay. The street names in Winnipeg's West Kildonan attest to their legacy, as does this recipe, found among the many handed down to Linda Furness, a descendant of the original settlers.

Oat Cakes   G. Gunn

1 egg
½ teas. salt
1 cup B. sugar
½ teas. soda dissolved in
                    hot water.

1 cup butter
3 cups R. Oats
1 cup flour   Roll, cut + bake.
Vanilla

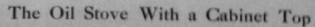
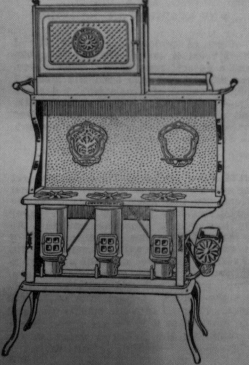
160

Matrimonial Cake

Nobody seems too sure why date squares are called
Matrimonial Cake in Manitoba but that is the
way I always knew them growing up. Someone once
suggested that the rough topping, sweet interior and
solid base might be a metaphor for marriage and that
sounds about right to me! I think Ruth Christie,
who donated this recipe, might even agree.

Matrimonial Squares

1½ lb of dates
1½ cups boiling water
Grated rind of 1 lemon
Juice of 1 lemon
2 cups sifted flour
¼ tsp salt
1 tsp baking powder
½ tsp baking soda
½ cup brown sugar
2½ cups quick cooking
rolled oats
1 cup butter

Add the boiling water and lemon rind to the
dates and cook over low heat until thickened.
Remove from stove and add the lemon juice.
Sift the flour, salt, baking powder, baking
soda and sugar together then add the rolled
oats. Cut in the butter with 2 knives or pastry
blender until mixture is crumbly. Spread half
of the flour mixture in a greased 12 x 8 x 2 pan
and press down. Pour the date mixture
over this and spread evenly. Cover the top
with the remaining flour mixture, patting
it to make it smooth. Bake in a moderate
oven at 350°F for 1 hour. Cool in the pan, then
cut into squares.

Wedding Cake

For more than 175 years, fruitcake was standard at many Manitoba weddings, a tradition brought over from Scotland by the Selkirk Settlers. Among them was Katherine McGillvary, who arrived in 1812, and John "Bushie" Matheson, who came in 1815 with his parents, Alexander and Ann Matheson of Sutherlandshire. These intrepid Scots were the ancestors of Linda Furness, who provided this recipe, handed down to her from her mother Mysie (Lindsay) Matheson.

WEDDING CAKE

12 eggs	1 whole nutmeg (grd)
1 lb. butter	3 tsp. mace (not level)
1½ lbs. powdered sugar	2 tsp. cinnamon (not level)
	1 tsp. allspice
3 lbs. seeded raisins (whole)	½ pint cream
2 lbs. sultanas	½ pint (wine & orange juice)
1 lb. currants	Rind of 2 oranges
1 lb. almonds	1 lb. citron peel
	1 lb flour.

If cherries are used, poke them in last.

Do not cut raisins. Prepare all fruit & have them dry. Dredge all fruit with part of measured flour. Beat sugar, butter to a very light cream. Add the well-beaten eggs, alternately with a little flour. Sift all spices & add them to cream and fruit juices. Then add to beaten mixture. Add remaining flour — a little at a time, alternately with fruit, stirring well & beating as hard as possible. Put in pans & bake slowly — 250' for 1 hr., 300' for 3 hrs. Total 4

This recipe was used for Jessie's wedding cake, also Aunt Jessie's and Grandma Matheson's Diamond Anniversary in 1935.

Imperial Christmas Cake

Imperial Christmas Cake   *Sultana*

1 lb white sugar	1 lb raisins
1 " flour	1 " butter.
3/4 lb blanched almonds	
3/4 " citron peel .	9. eggs.

Juice & grated rind of 1 lemon
Beat eggs. starting with a couple
& adding 1 at a time. Then cream
sugar & butter with eggs. add nut
peel & flour & bake in a slow oven

Amma Geysir's Vinarterta

"Takk Amma Geysir! A good Icelandic Vinarterta Recipe!"
This uniquely Icelandic cake dates back to the 19th century when white pastry flour became popular in Europe. Each pastry layer is baked separately, cooled, then spread and stacked. Because prunes preserve well, the filling was ideal for the early settlers of New Iceland who had little access to fresh fruit, including rhubarb, the traditional choice for vinarterta. A centrepiece of many-a-special occasion, vinarterta was best made in advance to allow moisture to penetrate the layers. Although it has fallen out of favour in its native land, it remains popular in Manitoba kitchens, bakeries, restaurants and farmers' markets. This recipe comes from Corrine Einarsson of Arborg, passed down from her grandmother, Amma Jonina Gislason from Geysir, Manitoba.

VINARTERTA:
½ cup soft butter
1 cup sugar
2 eggs
½ cup milk

1 teaspoon vanilla
Pinch of salt
3 cups flour
2 teaspoons baking powder

Cream butter and add sugar gradually. Add eggs, 1 at a time. Add milk and vanilla. Sift dry ingredients and add to first mixture. Knead in enough flour to make soft cookie dough. Divide into 6 equal parts and roll and cut with a 9-inch plate. Bake in a moderate oven at 375F until golden brown.

FILLING:
2 pounds prunes
2 cups water

¼ cup sugar
¼ teaspoon cardamom

Boil prunes and water until soft, then cool and stone. Grind prunes and whip them with sugar and cardamom.

164

Born in Baldur, Manitoba in 1905, the second child of Björn and Sigríður Dahlman, Anna Kristin 'Stina,' became renowned for her vinarterta, a recipe she passed down to her own daughter. Stina loved cooking and baking for her family and community. She took great care of both her own appearance and that of her baking. She is well-remembered in the community of Gimli where her grandson's wife opened a bakery that sells Vinarterta, made just the way Stina liked it!

Farm near Riverton

Amma Lauga Danielson's Kleinur

Kathy Thorsteinson remembers coming home from school to warm kleinur (pronounced klayner) fresh from the fryer when she lived at her Amma (Grandma) Lauga's house for three years as a child. Lauga came to New Iceland with her family when she was two. Kleinur are also known as love knots.

2 whole eggs
2 egg yolks
¾ cup sugar
½ cup butter, melted
½ cup cream

¼ teaspoon ground
  cardamom
1 teaspoon baking powder
3 cups flour
Oil for deep frying

Beat eggs until light, then beat in sugar. Add melted butter and cream. Add dry ingredients, using just enough flour so dough can be easily rolled out. Cut into diamond shapes using a fattigmann cutter. Cut slit in centre and pull lower tip of cookie through the slit. Deep-fry until light brown.

The easiest way to cut the dough for kleinur is to use a fattigmann cutter, a tool that simultaneously cuts the diamond shape and a slit in the middle of the diamond. No tool, no problem. Just use a pastry wheel. It will take a little longer but it works!

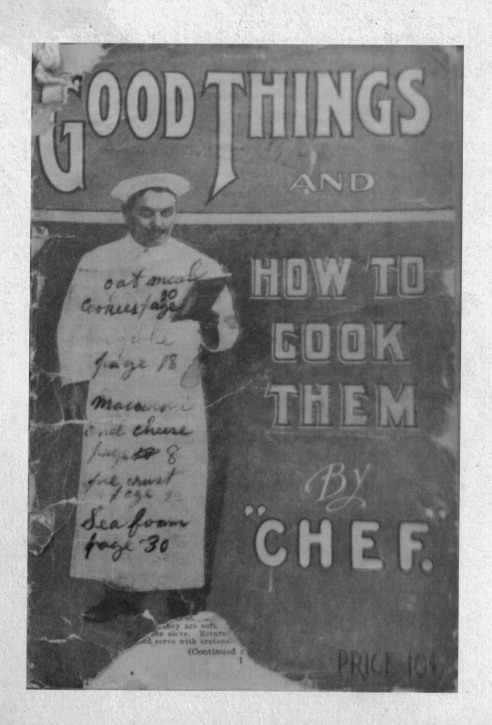

Aunt Adeline's Buttermilk Cake

Over the years, many churches published cookbooks with recipes collected from their parishioners to raise funds for renovations and special purchases such as organs. There were always a few pages in the back to add your own recipes – or those of Aunt Adeline.

Aunt Adeline's Buttermilk Cake

1½ cups Brown sugar
1 cup Butter
1½ cup Buttermilk
1 cup raisins
1 cup currents
3 cups flour
2 tps Baking powder
flavor with a little nutmeg
or other spice This makes
a good pudding buy
omiting the butter &
adding suet.

Another way to raise money for the church was the box social. Finger foods such as roast chicken, fresh bread, pickles and desserts were placed in decorated shoeboxes and auctioned off to the highest bidders. Each winner then had lunch with the one who prepared it.

Waffles and Vanilla Sauce

Mennonite women brought their waffle irons with them from Russia. The smaller ones were installed as an element in their wood-burning stoves but the larger 10-inch ones didn't fit. Composed of five joined hearts, these were used exclusively over an open fire.

2 cups flour	5 eggs
4 teaspoons baking powder	¼ cup butter, melted
½ teaspoon salt	1 cup milk

Mix flour, baking powder and salt. Beat eggs in a bowl and add flour mixture and melted butter. Add milk and stir until batter is smooth. Bake in waffle iron and serve with vanilla sauce.

VANILLA SAUCE:

2 cups light cream	4 tablespoons flour
¾ cup sugar	2 tablespoons butter
Pinch of salt	2 teaspoons vanilla

Mix cream, sugar and salt in a medium saucepan and heat just below boiling point. Remove from heat and add some of the liquid to the flour to make a thin paste. Add paste to the pot and stir. Return to heat and bring to a boil, stirring constantly. Take off heat and add butter and vanilla.

When using an
old-fashioned
cast iron waffle
maker, pour the
batter on the
sizzling bottom
surface, close
the lid and
immediately
turn the waffle
iron over so
the cooler side
starts to cook.

Bohémier-style Molasses Cookies

In the late 1880s, when Benjamin Bohémier and Marie-Louise Limoges-Bohémier moved from Quebec to start a 2,000-acre dairy farm in St. Norbert, they continued the French Canadian tradition of hosting the extended family on New Year's Eve. Even though the house was one of the largest in the area, it would take several sittings to feed the 21 Bohémier children and their families. Cookies, cakes and meat pies for the day were made and frozen weeks in advance. This recipe is taken from Culinary Heritage Gems of St. Norbert Pioneer Families.

½ cup butter
1 cup sugar
1 egg, well beaten
½ cup molasses
½ teaspoon vanilla
2 cups flour
2 teaspoons baking powder
1½ teaspoons baking soda
1 teaspoon ginger
1½ teaspoon cinnamon
½ teaspoon salt

In baking, using molasses was a common way to stretch the sweetness of sugar, which was expensive.

Cream butter and sugar. Add beaten egg, molasses and vanilla. Combine dry ingredients. Add to liquid mixture and mix well. Roll into small balls. Place on a greased cookie sheet about 2 inches apart as cookies will spread. Bake at 350F for 8 minutes. Makes 4 dozen cookies.

Aunt Mary's Cookies

Looks like Aunt Mary mixed her French and English along with her cookie dough. Here is a translation of the ingredients: 2 cups sugar, 4 well-beaten eggs, 2 teaspoons baking soda, 1 teaspoon salt, 2 cups butter, 5 cups flour, 4 teaspoons of cream of tartar. The essence is anyone's guess, but surely vanilla will do!

Aunt Mary's Cookies

2 t. sucre	5 t. farine
4 oeufs bien battus	4 c. à thé crême
2 c. à thé soda	de tartre
1 c. " " sel	essence
2 t. beurre	

Roll not too thin and sprinkle with sugar. Bake 10 min. in quick oven. Press a raisin in centre.

St. Norbert Family Dinner

Molasses Pulled Taffy
(Tire de la Sainte Catherine)

Corinne Dufort remembers pulling taffy with her Tante Lucille 'Lulu' Ouimet from St. Norbert in late November on 'la Sainte Catherine,' the day before Advent. The tradition originated in France and came to Manitoba with settlers from Quebec.

1 pound of brown sugar	½ cup water
1 cup molasses	2 tablespoons butter

Combine all ingredients in a pot and boil over high heat until the mixture hardens when dropped in cold water.

Pour the taffy into a large buttered platter or shallow pan. Rub butter over hands. When cool enough to handle, grab the edges with the tips of the fingers and thumbs. Pull slowly until your hands are 18 inches apart. Twist then fold by joining hands together. Do this a few times until the taffy holds its shape. Then pull apart until the rope is ½ to ¾-inch thick. Cut the rope every inch with buttered scissors onto a butter or sugar-covered surface.

Crêpes

Staunch Catholics, Franco-Manitobans observed a period of abstinence during Lent, which coincided with the depletion of their larder after a long winter. The day before the start of Lent, they celebrated Shrove Tuesday with a traditional feast of crêpes – thin pancakes served with maple syrup. In the evening, the children went door-to-door dressed in costumes, much like they now do at Halloween. They were treated to apples, candies and homemade fudge.

1½ teaspoon baking
   powder
1 tablespoon sugar
½ teaspoon salt
2 cups flour

2 cups milk
2 eggs
½ tablespoon butter,
   melted

Stir baking powder, sugar and salt into flour. Beat eggs, milk and melted butter in a separate bowl. Add to flour and mix well. Grease a pan with butter or lard and heat to medium high. Pour enough batter to spread a thin layer over the entire surface when you rotate the pan. The batter should set almost immediately. Flip the crêpe and cook the other side until golden.

IT IS SAID THAT THE FIRST CRÊPE TO HIT THE PAN, INVARIABLY A FLUB, IS FOR THE COOK TO EAT.

HAHA!
Poor Cook!

Sucre à la Crème

Many Métis eventually became dairy farmers, so cream was always available. Brought by the settlers from Québec, homemade fudge became a favourite treat. This recipe adapted from Culinary Heritage Gems of St. Norbert Pioneer Families includes maple sugar, but doubling the brown sugar works, too.

1 cup brown sugar, packed
1 cup maple sugar
½ cup 18% cream

2 tablespoons butter
½ teaspoon vanilla
1 cup nuts, chopped (optional)

In a heavy sauce pan, bring sugars and cream just to the boiling point, stirring constantly. Boil without stirring for 5 minutes or until mixture forms a ball when dropped in cold water. Remove from heat and add butter and vanilla. Cool to lukewarm. Beat for 2 to 3 minutes until thick. Quickly stir in nuts (if using) and pour into a buttered pan. Score while cool. Cut when cold.

The W.T. Rawleigh Company Canada's first large manufacturing plant of spices, essences and vanilla opened in Winnipeg in 1902.

Platz

Along with this traditional version, adapted from
The Mennonite Treasury of Recipes, Karen Martens of
Neubergthal also makes 'pie-by-the-yard,' a popular
Manitoba adaptation for large gatherings. For 'pie-by-the-
yard' she replaces the bottom layer with a simple shortening
and flour pie crust, which makes it quicker to prepare several
cookie sheets of pastries at a time. Either version can be
made with any fruit in season, but rhubarb is a favourite.

2 cups flour
3 teaspoons baking powder
4 tablespoons sugar

2 tablespoons shortening
   (butter or lard)
½ cup cream
1 egg

Mix all ingredients well. Pat out on a fairly large greased
baking sheet, pushing up sides. Put on a layer of any
fruit in season. This recipe should handle about 2 cups
fruit mixed with ½ cup sugar.

TOP WITH RUEBEL:
¾ cup sugar
¾ cup flour
½ teaspoon baking powder

2 tablespoons butter
A bit of cream

Mix first 3 ingredients well, then
rub in the butter and enough
cream to make coarse crumbs
or ruebel. Sprinkle thickly over
fruit and bake at 375F for 25 to
30 minutes.

A national historic site,
Neubergthal is a street village
with long narrow farmsteads
extending behind the homes.
The Manitoba government
allowed the first Mennonite
immigrants to settle in village
communities, as they had
done in Europe, rather than on
dispersed homesteads.

Peppernuts

Food writer Doris Penner describes peppernuts as a popular Mennonite Christmas cookie with Dutch overtones. She notes that in early days, spices were expensive and oftentimes unavailable. Pepper was sometimes added to cinnamon, cloves and ginger to accentuate and thereby stretch the taste.

2 cups corn syrup
1 cup sugar
¾ cup butter, melted
2 eggs
½ cup buttermilk or
  sour milk

1 teaspoon baking soda
  (dissolve in buttermilk)
6 cups flour
1 teaspoon each:
  cinnamon and cloves
½ teaspoon each: ground
  star anise and ginger

Combine syrup and sugar in mixing bowl. Stir in melted butter and beat in eggs, one at a time. Add buttermilk with baking soda to mixture. In separate bowl, mix flour and spices and gradually add to liquid mixture. Knead well. Cover and chill for a few hours or overnight. Roll dough into pencil thin strips and slice into ¼-inch thick small coins. Place on greased baking sheet. Bake at 350F for 7 to 8 minutes or until golden brown. Cool and store in airtight container.

Early recipes produced hard cookies that stored well, with softer versions evolving over time. Doris' recipe is for the original peppernuts and therefore hard to the bite.

Jam Busters

For decades, Manitobans have had a soft spot for jelly doughnuts, which they call jam busters. Could it be because they
were the preferred pastry of Polish settlers? Or did their popularity originate with a version cherished by Jewish immigrants at
Hanukkah? Here is a recipe for the Polish version called paczki.

1 teaspoon sugar
¼ cup warm water
2¼ teaspoons yeast
12 egg yolks
1 teaspoon salt
⅓ cup rum
1 cup cream

⅓ cup butter
½ cup sugar
4½ cups flour
1½ cups jam
Oil or lard for deep frying
Powdered sugar

In a small bowl, dissolve sugar in warm water. Sprinkle
yeast on water and let rest until foamy, about 10 minutes.
Meanwhile, beat egg yolks with salt in another small bowl
until thick and pale. Stir in rum and cream.

In a large bowl, cream butter. Add sugar gradually,
beating until fluffy. Slowly beat in yeast mixture. Add flour,
one cup at a time, alternately with the egg mixture. Turn
out on floured surface and knead for 5 minutes. Return to
bowl, cover with a damp towel and let rise about 30 minutes.
When doubled in size, roll out to a thickness of ¾ inch on
a floured surface. Cut in rounds with a 3-inch cookie cutter
or glass.

Place 1 tablespoon of jam in the centre of half the
circles. Top each with a circle and seal well, pinching the
edges. Cover loosely with a floured towel and let rise for
20 minutes.

Deep fry in hot fat or oil until golden brown on both
sides. Remove and roll in powdered sugar. Cool thoroughly
before eating.

Walnut Bake and English Raisin Bake

Walnut Cake.

2 eggs

1 cup Sugar

½ " Butter

1 " Rasins

1 " Walnuts

1 " Sweet Milk

2 " Flour

2 tea spoons B. Powder.

English Rasin Cake.

1 cup G. Sugar } creamed together

½ " Butter

½ " Milk

1 " Rasins

1 " Chopped Walnuts

3 " Flour

2 eggs well beaten

2 teaspoons B. Powder

Our People, Our Food

Mennonite East Reserve

After Dr. Katharina Thiessen delivered a baby, she would stay with the family for a few days, cleaning and cooking while the mother and the newborn rested. It is not surprising, then, that along with 399 recipes for medicines, balms and poultices, her notebook also includes a recipe for relish. The Mennonite doctor and midwife set down roots in 1885 in Manitoba's West Reserve, an area just north of the U.S. border, between Emerson on the Red River and Mountain City near the Pembina Hills. She found a thriving community eager for her services and skills.

"One of the first things the midwife did was to put the kettle on to boil," recalls Alma Barkman in Mennonite Memories of Settling in Canada. "Then father would be told to go to the henhouse for the fattest chicken. Not long after, there would be chicken noodle soup bubbling on the stove."

A unique version of the soup, spiced with star-anise, is one of many distinctive recipes influenced by the Mennonites' migration from the German and Dutch-speaking parts of Europe as they escaped religious persecution. Eventually, a large group relocated to Ukraine and Russia. While adapting to local ingredients, they held on to many traditional ways of preparing food, a vital part of preserving their culture and identity in a new land. As a result, food from Russian Mennonites who immigrated to Manitoba may share some similarities with Ukrainian fare, but has its own distinctive affinities for such flavours as cream, pepper and anise.

Mennonites arrive

In 1875, encouraged by Canada's promise of religious freedom, exemption from military service and control over their own schools, 1,533 Mennonite men, women and children from Ukraine settled in an area east of the Red River. They established 21 villages in what was named the East Reserve, including Steinbach, now Manitoba's third largest city. In 1875, another 3,341 joined them, representing 12 percent of total Canadian immigration that year. With arable land running out in the East Reserve, immigrants from this second wave secured 50,000 acres in the Pembina Hills, an area they called the West Reserve. In total, about 7,000 Mennonites had settled in Manitoba by 1880. Subsequent waves would follow including a large exodus from Russia in the 1920s after the Bolshevik Revolution.

Skilled farmers, the Mennonites focused on producing food. The early settlers acquired Red River carts and filled them with tools and implements purchased in Winnipeg, along with cook stoves and kitchen utensils. The first meals were prepared around these wagons, as construction and farming began. Before long, the stove was moved from the semlin or sod house into a typical wooden Mennonite farmhouse connected to the barn, making it easy to feed the animals and collect the eggs for cooking, even on the coldest winter day.

Manitoba's population of hogs and chickens also increased during those years, fulfilling the need for two key ingredients in Mennonite cooking. After all, what was dinner without farmer's sausage and kielke, those lovely soft egg noodles with cream sauce? What was Sunday Faspa without a slice of sweet platz?

THE FASPA MEAL

Served every afternoon around 3 pm as a break from work, the traditional Faspa meal consisted of bread, jam, cheese, pickles and preserves. Then there was Sunday Faspa, a special time when families visited one another after church to enjoy a strong coffee with zwieback buns, cakes and cookies.

Likely, it would have been the midwife who helped prepare that first Faspa to introduce a newborn to the community after the birth. The village women would come laden with meals for the family, including their own homemade chicken noodle soup. Fortified by this nourishing food, the mother would be strong enough to receive her guests and enjoy a slice of rhubarb platz right along with them.

Midwives had a special role in Mennonite life. It was a shock to the community when, in 1895, doctors from the town of Morden and the College of Physicians and Surgeons tried to charge Katharina Thiessen for practicing without a licence so they could better profit from providing medical services to the West Reserve. On the third try they succeeded. But when MLA Valentine Winkler paid Katharina's $50 fine and threatened to pass a bill exempting the Mennonites from provisions of the Medical Act, the litigants backed down. As a result, new mothers in the West Reserve continued to benefit from the post-natal care and cooking only a midwife was willing to provide.

A HIGH QUALITY PRODUCT

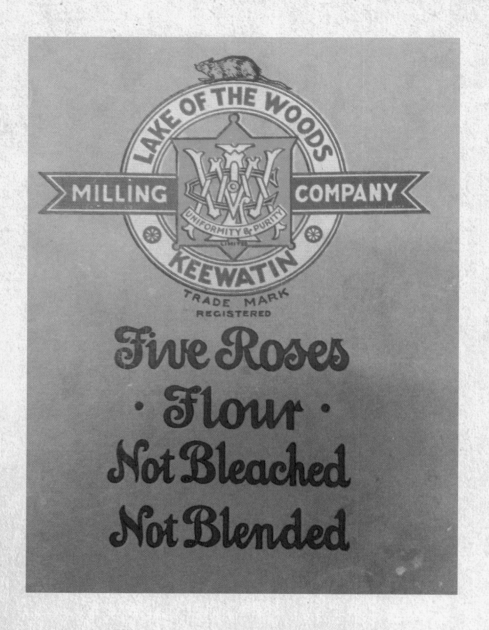

Puddings and Pies

"Three hours will be, as a rule, the longest time required for the boiling of a pudding of ordinary size. All boiled puddings should be served as soon as they are cooked." – Five Roses Cook Book (1915)

Puddings and pies, the humble cousins of cakes and cookies, could be made with little fuss from whatever was on hand. Ah, pie! Freshly-picked wild saskatoons, strawberries, raspberries, cranberries and blueberries enclosed in a pastry crust made for a simple sweet ending to any meal. Gardening increased the options with pie fillings such as rhubarb in the summertime and pumpkin in the fall. Most home cooks needed no recipe for the pastry. After years of practice, preparing the crust became second nature.

A gathering of pies

Pies were a favourite for large gatherings and picnics because they could be made easily in large quantities and transported in their tins. Manitoba Mennonites even developed a square version of the traditionally round dessert, pie-by-the-yard featuring almost any fruit – plums, apples, raspberries, blueberries, apricot – or any combination thereof.

Not all pies were fruit. French Canadian transplants to Manitoba favoured sugar pie, often substituting brown sugar for the hard-to-find maple syrup they had used in Quebec. Nor were their pies always sweet. Along with tourtière or meat pie, Franco-Manitobans layered potatoes, onion, rabbit, chicken, pork, beef, venison, grouse – basically any meat available – between six sheets of pastry in a dish aptly-named 'six pâtes.' This was corrupted to cipâtes and then cipailles, becoming "sea pie" when it made its way to English kitchens.

"I remember when we were at Miss Davis' Boarding school, often having to eat sturgeon and sea pie," writes Jean Drever of growing up in Fort Garry in the 1860s. When meat was scarce, any scrap was a candidate for this versatile dish.

Thrifty cooks also knew how to turn stale bread crumbs and suet into tasty steamed puddings. When even those ingredients were scarce, carrots made a moist and delicious substitute. A well-made sauce could turn any pudding into a delicious treat.

A welcomed treat

When times were good, puddings were endowed with currants and raisins, maybe even a chopped apple and some citron peel. Or those ingredients were saved for special occasions such as Christmas and New Year's. Served warm, pudding was always a welcome treat in the depth of a Manitoba winter.

Ingredients for some sort of boiled pudding were almost always on hand. So was a good mold with a tight fitting lid or, at the very least, a lard pail with a top that could be tied on. A few hours later, dessert was ready to serve!

Steam Pudding

Steam pudding.
2 cups flour
1 cup sweet milk
1 cup sugar
½ cup meat
1 egg
1 tea spoon soda
1 cup raisins
1 cup currants
put in bag & steam
2 hours in steamer
covered tight.

Suet Pudding

1 cup suet minced fine
2 cups flour
2 " bread Crumb dried & run through
meat grinder
1 cup sugar
1 ts heaping Baking Powder
1 cup milk
2 " raisins
1 " Currants
½ ts salt
1 ts cinnamon
½ " cloves
½ " nutmeg
½ allspice

Boil 3 hrs, you may use a small sugar
bag dipped in boiling water & then in
flour so it wont stick to bag

191

Sauce for Pudding

Sauce for pudding
1 cup Brown sugar mix
smooth in a little milk
2 table spoons flour
1 table " butter.
add 2 cups boiling water
add butter, salt, flavoring
vinegar

192

Blueberry Slump

Summertime meant berry picking for Ruth Christie
and her family when she was a young girl living in
Loon Straits. Although blueberries are most abundant
in the eastern part of the province on the edge of the
Canadian Shield, there are bountiful patches along
the shores of Lake Winnipeg for those who know where
to find them. Ruth remembers long hot summer days
spent picking on Black Island. Store-bought blueberries will work fine for this recipe but Ruth will tell you
that nothing compares to the sweetness of wild berries for
creating delicious desserts.

Blueberry Slump
1 qt blueberries
½ cup water   boil in a heavy saucepan
1½ cups sugar
1 tsp nutmeg
Batter
1 cup flour
1 tsp baking powder
1 tbsp sugar
¼ tsp. salt
1 egg
3 tbsp milk
2 tbsp melted fat
Sift dry ingredients, combine egg, milk and
melted fat and add to the flour mixture,
stirring just until dry ingredients moistened.
Drop batter mixture by spoonfuls on boiling
berries. Cover and cook 10 minutes. Serve hot
with cream.

Plum Pudding

In 1870, Jean Drever and her family were living near Upper Fort Garry. In her memoir, she recalls the Christmas during the Red River Rebellion when her sister Mary made six plum puddings for those imprisoned in the Fort by Louis Riel and his men.

```
                CHRISTMAS PLUM PUDDING
     1 cup Flour
     1 cup Gran. Sugar
     1 cup Suet
     1 cup Raisins or dates      1 teasp. Cassia or
     1 cup Currants              1 teasp. Nutmeg
     1 CUP MIXED PEEL            1 teasp. Soda
     1 cup chopped apples
     1 cup milk
     1 cup bread crumbs
   Walnuts or Almonds
   (Peel may be omitted.)

   Boil 3 hours.
```

Carrot Pudding

Carrots were often in abundance as they were easy to grow in prairie gardens. Virtually every family had their variation of carrot pudding.

Carrot pudding
1 cup carrots grated raw
1 cup potatoes grated raw
1 cup brown sugar
1 cup suet
1 cup raisins (currants)
a little peel (Salt)
2 cups flour
1 tsp Baking soda
dissolve in a little
water steam 3 hours.

Preparing berries

Mock Cherry Pie

There were no cherries in Manitoba, but the forest did provide both highbush and lowbush cranberries. Despite the name, they are not cranberries at all but a local plant with similar tart red berries. Nonetheless, they do make for a delicious substitute.

Pastry for two pie shells
1 cup highbush or
    lowbush cranberries
    (true cranberries will
    work fine)
½ cup water
1 cup sugar
1 teaspoon vanilla
1 tablespoon flour
1 egg

Cook berries in water until they pop. If using wild berries, strain through a sieve or vegetable mill into a saucepan, then discard seeds and skins. Add remaining ingredients and mix well, cooking over medium heat until thickened. Pour into unbaked pie shell. Cover with 1/4-inch strips of pie dough in a lattice pattern. Bake at 375F for 40 minutes.

In Women of Red River, Mrs. William Logan relates how the wives of the English-speaking settlers brought roast beef, bread, cakes and pies to the men imprisoned in Fort Garry by Louis Riel and his men during the rebellion. When Canadian troops arrived in the summer of 1870, she baked every day, turning an entire bag of flour into bread and buns, which her little boy took to sell to the soldiers.

Sugar Pie/Tarte au Sucre

No maple syrup, no problem! Resourceful Franco-Manitobans had a solution: increase the brown sugar to two cups and double the cream. Here is the unaltered recipe.

Pastry for a single-crust
   8-inch pie
½ cup light brown sugar
2 large eggs

½ cup heavy cream
⅓ cup pure maple syrup
2 teaspoons butter,
   melted

Heat the oven to 350F. Beat brown sugar and eggs until creamy. Stir in cream, syrup (if using) and butter until smooth. Pour into prepared pie shell. Bake on lower third of oven until pastry is golden, approximately 50 to 60 minutes. Filling will still be soft but will set as the pie cools.

Tarte à la Ferlouche

In the middle of winter it was always possible to find molasses and some stray raisins to make a pie. Also known as farlouche or fanfarlouche, this is a French-Canadian favourite.

1 baked 9-inch
   pie shell
1 cup molasses
1 cup water
½ cup flour

½ cup raisins
1 tablespoon butter
Whipped cream and
   chopped nuts
   (optional)

Combine molasses, water and flour in a medium saucepan. Cook until creamy. Add raisins and continue cooking until transparent, about 10 minutes. Remove from heat, add butter and stir until melted. Pour into baked pie shell and let cool. Top with whipped cream, flavoured with brandy if desired. Sprinkle with chopped nuts.

Sour Cream Pie

Sour Cream Pie.

1 cup of sour cream.
3/4 cup of sugar.
Yolks of two eggs, well beaten
3/4 cup of seeded raisins
Cinnamon, cloves, allspice, boil it
a few minutes and pour it into
a lower crust. put whites of eggs on
top. very rich, but good for those
that are fond of sweet things.

200

Chiffon Pie

An American dessert invented in the 1920s, chiffon pie became all the rage north of the border.

Chiffon Pie —
mix 1 1/4 sugar, 1/2 cup Flour
1/2 tea sp. Salt, 1 1/4 cups B.
water stir constantly & cook
15 min. add juice & rind
1 large orange, juice 1 lemon
3 well beaten yolks of eggs
cook until thick cool &
a meringue of whites 3 eggs
sugar & lemon & orange juice
put 1/4 of whites into custard
turn into a baked pie
shell & cover with un-
meran — & brown — .

P.S This is delectable

201

Saskatoon Pie

An early summer fruit, saskatoons were a staple for Manitoba's Indigenous people and later, the early settlers. Rich in vitamin C, the purple berries were eaten fresh or dried for preservation. The word saskatoon comes from the Cree name: "mis-sask-quah-too-mina."

Pastry for a two-crust
   9-inch pie.
3 cups saskatoons
2 tablespoons flour

½ cup sugar
¼ teaspoon nutmeg or
   cardamom (optional)
2 tablespoons lemon juice

Mix all ingredients in a bowl and pour into a pastry crust. Cover with second crust and vent with five small slits. Bake at 425F for 10 minutes. Reduce heat to 350F and bake 35 minutes longer. Cool before serving. Delicious eaten with vanilla ice cream.

During his time in Manitoba, David Thompson identified 20 species of native berries, including strawberries, bearberries, bunchberries, saskatoons, chokecherries and two different kinds of raspberries.

What a relief! Finally, Yevdokia Smerechanski no longer had to walk three kilometres to bake bread in her neighbour's outdoor oven. In *Toil and Triumph: The Lives and Times of Anton and Yevdokia Smerechanski, Pioneer Ukrainian Settlers of Manitoba's Interlake*, Olenka Negrych relates how this Ukrainian settler went to great lengths to feed her family. Several months later, she had her own "pich" (pronounced peach), a metre-high straw and clay dome oven on a cement slab, in which to cook everything from paska to pyrohy.

After building a roaring fire in the pich, a vent was opened to bring the temperature down. It was important to start with whatever needed the most cooking, such as cabbage rolls, and work your way down to lighter fare, with the bread last. At Easter that would be the paska, a rich round loaf adorned with elaborate dough ornaments in the shape of braids, birds and crosses, which was then brought to the church for blessing.

UKRAINIANS ARRIVE

In 1896, Canada's Minister of Immigration, Clifford Sifton turned to Europe for "a stalwart peasant in a sheepskin coat, born on the soil, whose forefathers have been farmers for 10 generations, with a stout wife and a half-dozen children." By bringing Ukrainians to Manitoba, Sifton introduced the provincial palate to new tastes and preparations, including a legacy of kielbasa (sausage), cabbage rolls and perogies (also known as pyrohy) that has persisted to this day.

The following year, in the first large wave of immigration, 4,000 Ukrainians passed through the Canadian Pacific Railway station in Winnipeg on their way to homesteads across the province, from Vita and Gardenton to Teulon, Dauphin, Gilbert Plains and everywhere in between. In subsequent years, they were followed by thousands more, tilling the soil to turn the prairie into a vast sea of wheat. Along with immigrants from Poland and other parts of Europe, they helped transform the prairies into the breadbasket of Canada.

Wheat holds a special place in Ukrainian culture. Before the table is set on Christmas Eve, straw is spread on the floor and a sheaf of wheat (didukh) is displayed in a corner of the dining room. Three loaves of round braided bread or kolach, each adorned with a candle, serve as the centrepiece on the dining table.

To this day, many Manitobans of Ukrainian heritage

continue to observe the custom of serving 12 meatless and milkless dishes for the holy meal on Christmas Eve. The meal always starts with kutya, a mixture of cooked wheat, honey, ground poppy seeds and chopped nuts. Next comes a special meatless borscht laced with small triangular-shaped pieces of dough — and no sour cream, it's Christmas! Then come the pyrohy — filled with anything from mushrooms and sauerkraut to poppyseeds and raisins — followed by beans, fish served three ways, cabbage rolls, mushrooms in sauce, stewed dried fruit, deep fried pastries and a tall layer cake with prunes. What a spread!

Among all ethnic groups, food is central to a celebration, and Ukrainians are no exception. Manitobans are all familiar with the ubiquitous 'lunch' at the end of the wedding social: pickles, kielbasa sausage, cheese, mustard and — of course — rye bread, served at midnight, after hours of dancing and libation. No one seems to be quite sure about the origin of these social events celebrating the future bride and groom months before the wedding. But it certainly looks like there's a Ukrainian connection somewhere!

Ukrainian Farm near Fraserwood

Pickles
and Preserves

"Have nuts to pull also, red cabbage to pickle and beets." – Belle Chew, Elkhorn, Manitoba

In 1890, Belle Chew, wrote in a letter to her uncle in Scotland that she has been "busy pulling and preserving fruit for winter" including saskatoons, raspberries and black currants with which to make jams, jellies and vinegars. Highbush cranberries were always last to 'pull' or pick as they are the last fruit in the forest to ripen, ready for picking around the same time as wild hazelnuts, just before the first frost.

This was the time of year when women on the prairies were preoccupied with preserving and pickling the produce from their gardens to carry their families through the winter. Belle tells her uncle she has preserved a jar of green peas, a treat since most of the peas were dried and destined for the soup pot.

Meanwhile red cabbage, beets and cucumbers were pickled, sometimes by themselves, sometimes as mixed pickles in recipes that have been passed on through generations. Belle's composition included cucumbers, peas, onions, radish pods and mango melons.

A touch of salt

No matter what the recipe, salt was the a vital ingredient for anyone 'putting up' quart sealers of preserved vegetables in the pantry or down in the root cellar beside barrels of apples, bags of potatoes and cases of carrots buried in sand. Back when the HBC was the only game in town, salt was expensive, with much of it reserved for salting meat or fish.

Then there were the Monkmans, descendants of Englishman James Monkman and his Cree wife Mary. Indigenous elder Ruth Christie relates that, in the early 1800s, one of her ancestors, Joseph

"Old Joe" Monkman, started production at Salt Springs on the northwest shore of Lake Winnipegosis. He and his sons collected brine from the naturally flowing springs and boiled it in four-by-five-foot iron pans atop a rough stone fireplace until the water evaporated, leaving behind the white crystals of salt. The salt was stored in birch bark 'rogans' carried by York boat and oxcart to communities as far as Portage La Prairie, more than 300 kilometres away. A bushel of salt — just a little more than 30 quarts — cost $1.25. Each York boat could carry 90 bushels. In 1874, more than 1,000 bushels of salt were shipped each year from the Monkman springs. Families such as the Campbells also became involved in large-scale salt operations. Manitoba's production came to a halt when the railway arrived, bringing cheaper salt from Ontario.

A splash of vinegar

Vinegar was another essential ingredient for preserving food, particularly for pickling vegetables. Long before the wagon trade started to consistently bring goods from south of the border along the Pembina and Crow Wing Trails (now Highways 75 and 59), the Métis became adept at making vinegar from chokecherries or maple sap. However, by the time Ukrainian and Polish settlers arrived, there was plenty of cheap vinegar available in country stores to make their beloved garlic dill pickles, a fixture to this day at the lunch that marks the end of every good Manitoba social.

United Vinegar Works in Gimli, Manitoba

Bean Pickles

This recipe is from Phyllis Fraser, whose mother is a direct descendant of the Selkirk Settlers.

<u>BEAN PICKLES</u>

1 peck butter beans   Boil with a good deal of salt & drain well.

<u>Dressing</u>
3 pts. Vinegar
2½ lbs. white sugar
1 tab. tumeric
2 tab. celery Seed
1 teacup Flour
1 teacup Mustard
Boil till well cooked & pour over beans.
Bottle when cold.

In Scotland, the peck was used as a dry measure until the introduction of Imperial units in 1824, well after Thomas Douglas, the Earl of Selkirk, implemented his plan to resettle the Scottish crofters in Manitoba. A peck is equal to approximately 2 gallons or 32 cups. A simple rule of thumb: 2 cups in a pint, 2 pints in a quart, 4 quarts in a gallon.

Eyjofsson General Store

Sweet Green Tomato Pickles

"One of Mom's great pickle recipes; you always have too many green tomatoes and this uses lots," writes Pat Eyolfson, a descendant of the first Icelandic Settlers in the area. As a key driver behind the creation of the Arborg & District Multicultural Heritage Village, Eyolfson helped put together a community cookbook to raise funds for the project. In 2016, she was recognized with the Lieutenant Governor's Manitoba History Award for historical preservation and promotion.

12 medium-sized onions
8 quarts green tomatoes
Salt
1½ quarts white vinegar

12 cups brown sugar
3 tablespoons pickling spice

Peel onions and place in cold water. Wash and slice the tomatoes. Put ¼ of tomatoes in a large crock. Slice 3 of the onions very thin and place on top of tomatoes. Spread with 3 tablespoons of salt. Repeat this process until onions and tomatoes are used up. Weigh down with a plate and let stand overnight.

In the morning, drain well and rinse with hot water. In a large pot, heat vinegar to boiling point. Add sugar, then spices in a cheesecloth bag. Add tomato and onion mixture and cook slowly 1 to 1½ hours until tomatoes become clear. Remove spices. Seal in sterile jars.

In Women of Red River, Mrs. Robert James Henderson, born in Kildonan, tells W.J. Healy that she saw a ripe tomato for the first time in 1874. It took years before the settlers were able to import or develop a varietal that would ripen within the short growing season.

Farm garden in Gladstone

214

Cabbage Pickles

This recipe comes from one of the first recipe books published in Manitoba, Mother's Cook Book, probably created by Winnipeg chemist, J.H. Rose, to drum up business for some of his products, including pepper and vinegar.

1 quart raw cabbage (white), finely chopped
2 cups sugar
1 tablespoon salt
1 teaspoon black pepper
¼ teaspoon red pepper
1 cup grated
    horseradish

Combine all ingredients in a large crock. Cover with cold vinegar and keep from air.

For this medley — more relish than pickle — "keep from air" meant ladle into sterilized jars and seal.

Dill Pickles

Tina Grieve was lucky to have been born in 1875 or she would have had to pack her dill pickles in crockery. The mason jar was invented in the late 1860s and quickly made its way to Red River. Until then, crockery was the way to go and that's what the Mennonites used for their dill cukes, placing oak leaves on top to keep them crisp!

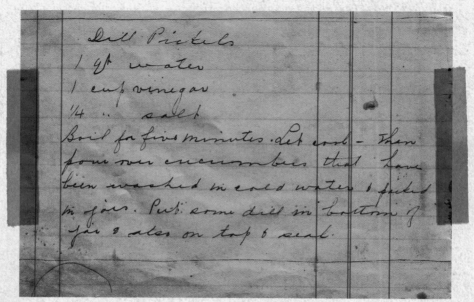

Ukrainian Dill and Garlic Pickles

Garlic came to Manitoba with Ukrainian immigrants who used it liberally in their cooking and preserves. Until then, it was practically an unknown ingredient in Manitoba kitchens.

5 pounds small
  cucumbers
1 large bunch fresh
  dill sprigs
Cloves from 2 bulbs of
  garlic, peeled

1 tablespoon whole
  peppercorns
4 quarts water
¾ cup pickling salt

Cover cucumbers in cold water and soak overnight. Sterilize 4 quart jars. Trim the ends of the cucumbers and make a small slit lengthwise with a sharp knife. Divide the garlic cloves, peppercorns and dill sprigs into 8 piles. Place one pile in the bottom of each quart jar. Fill with cucumbers. Top each jar with one of the remaining piles. Combine the water and salt in a large pot, bring to a boil, then pour into each jar to cover cucumbers. Seal and process.

The importance of bringing in people to grow food was promoted by the Manitoba Department of Agriculture and Immigration, publisher of the Manitoba Farmers' Library, an annual booklet filled with advice on canning, pickling and preserving food.

Bread and Butter Pickles

Bread and Butter Pickles

8 medium cucumbers
4 onions sliced
1 tbsp pickling salt
1 1/4 c. vinegar
1 1/2 c. sugar
1 tsp. celery and mustard seeds
1/2 tsp turmeric

Scrub cucumbers. Slice. Pare
onions. Cut into slices. Place
remaining ingredients in pot.
Bring to boil. Add cucumbers and
onions. Bring to boil. Turn heat
to medium. Cook 2 min. Put in
sterilized jars. About 4 pts.

Watermelon Pickles

The Mennonites were very fond of watermelon and grew it in abundance. In the fall, there were always a few stragglers left in the garden. If they were small enough, they were pickled whole. If not, they were cut into generous chunks and packed into large crocks. Today, we would use quart jars. This recipe is adapted from the Mennonite Cookbook compiled by the Altona Women's Institute.

Watermelon chunks
   to fill 6 quart jars
1-2 sprigs of dill
   per quart

2 cups sugar
1 cup white vinegar
½ cup pickling salt

Cut watermelon into large chunks and place in sterilized jars with one sprig of dill on top. Combine sugar, vinegar and salt in a saucepan and boil for 5 minutes. Pour over watermelon. Close jars and process for 10 to 15 minutes in a hot water bath to seal.

Altona is known as the Sunflower Capital for growing the tasty seeds or 'knackzoat,' a favourite Mennonite — and now Manitoban — snack.

My favourite!!!

Raw Sauce

Raw Sauce
1 peck ripe tomatoes
4 bunches celery
12 large onions
2 red peppers
all chopped together
let stand over night
if any water rises drain
off them add 4 table
spoons cinnamon
2 table spoons ground cloves
2 " " Black pepper
1 " " red pepper
2 cups brown sugar
2 cups salt   Bottle for use
2 quarts of vinegar

Governor's Sauce

This recipe, from the Western Farmers' Handbook, is one of many handwritten and printed versions of this sauce found in turn-of-the-century kitchens.

One peck green tomatoes, four large onions, six red peppers, one teacup grated horseradish, one teaspoon cayenne and one of black pepper, 1 teaspoon mustard, ½ cup sugar; slice tomatoes and sprinkle 1 teacup salt and lay all night, drain well then simmer till cooked through.

Early cookbook recipes often assumed the home cook would understand all the steps involved, so they weren't spelled out.

For this recipe, chop the onions and peppers, and, before simmering, be sure all the ingredients are in the pot!

Raspberry Vinegar

Rasberry vinegar
Put 4 quarts of berries in
a Kettle with enough vinegar to
cover let stand 2 hrs then
scald. stain & add 1 pint
sugar to every pint of Juce
boil 20 min & bottle.
                    Mrs H. A. Leslie

Suppsel

Chokecherries have always grown in abundance throughout much of Manitoba so they were easy pickings for the province's pioneers. The dark purple berries get their name from the way they dry out your mouth and make you pucker. Because they have a large seed in the middle, they are useless for pies but the juice is great for jelly or this runny Mennonite jam served with rollkuchen or as a dipping for bread at Faspa.

    4 quarts chokecherries
    3 cups water
    6 cups sugar

Combine chokecherries and water in a saucepan. Bring to a boil. Simmer till cherries have popped (about 20 to 25 minutes), stirring occasionally. Strain through sieve, preserving the liquid and discarding the flesh and pits. Add sugar to liquid and cook for another 30 minutes on low heat until mixture slightly thickens, stirring frequently. Pour into hot sterilized jars and seal. Store in a cool dark dry place.

Eating Jam!

Wild Plum Jam

Although newcomers to Manitoba found no apples
or pears growing in their adopted homeland, their
Indigenous neighbours introduced them to an abundance of wild fruit and berries. In the forest, plums
start to ripen in late August.

4 cups plums　　　　　　3 cups sugar
2 teaspoons soda　　　　3 cups water
1 quart water

Wash plums. Cook in a mixture of water and soda
for 10 minutes. Drain well. Return to the pot,
adding three cups water. Bring to a boil and add
sugar. Stir constantly, removing all stones as they rise
to the top. Cook until thick. Pour into sterilized jars
and seal.

Rose Hip Jelly

Rose hips are very high in vitamin C but very low in pectin. In mid-summer, early settlers and homesteaders used dried apples left over from the past winter (which are full of natural pectin) to give the jelly a firmer consistency.

> 1 quart dried apple slices
> 1 quart fresh rose hips
> 2 cups sugar

In a large pot, cover dried apples with warm water and soak overnight. Add 1 quart fresh rose hips and enough water to cover. Bring to a boil and cook until fruit is soft. Drain liquid through a cloth bag into a clean pot.

Add sugar and boil for 20 minutes or until a spoonful of mixture forms a thick mass when dropped into cold water.

Pour into sterilized jars and seal.

Our People, Our Food

Winnipeg General Strike

"No Need to Hunger" read the headline in the Western
Labour News on May 31, 1919. "The Women's Labor League
is doing splendid work through their restaurant adjoining the Strathcona Hotel. . . No one need want.
. . Strikers, get your meals at the Labor League
Restaurant. If you can pay for them do so. If you
can't you are welcome."

Two weeks earlier, more than 30,000 Winnipeggers
had walked off the job in what proved to be the largest
strike in Canadian history. The striking men were
joined by a large contingent of women — telephone
operators, stenographers, waitresses, laundresses, con-
fectionary workers, etc. — led by the president of the
Women's Labor League, Helen Armstrong, a.k.a, the "Wild
Woman of the West."

"It is impossible for a girl to live in a decent
and healthy manner under $10 a week," Mrs. Armstrong
told The Voice, one of Winnipeg's primary sources of

labour news. At the time, single working women received an average weekly wage of $5. The very act of going on strike meant they would go hungry.

Trust a wife and mother to realize it's hard to walk a picket line on an empty stomach! In no time, Mrs. Armstrong rose to the challenge, spearheading the formation of a labour café in the Strathcona Hotel at the corner of Rupert and Main. It was there that the Women's League and its sympathizers set up the first food kitchen for their striking sisters. Meals were funded by the Relief Committee, which collected donations from strikers meeting across the city and from fundraising activities such as dances. At the same time, another mouthpiece for the movement, The Western Labor News, published appeals for donations of bread, tea, sugar, vegetables and sandwiches.

Soup and sandwiches were staples, as they could be made in large quantities and were ready to serve at a moment's notice to waves of strikers passing through the doors. Although the soup kitchens were mainly run by women for women, men were also welcome. However, they were expected to make a donation or pay for their meals. If unable to contribute, they could obtain a special ticket from the relief committee and get their meals for free.

LABOUR LEAGUE CAFÉ

Not long after opening in the Strathcona, the Labor League Café was forced to relocate due to pressure from the Winnipeg businessman who owned the mortgage on the hotel. Operations then moved to the Royal Albert and then to the Oxford Hotel, which proved to be a fortuitous upgrade from the Strathcona. Thanks to Oxford's large dining room and modern kitchen, as many as 1,500 free meals were served daily to the men and women on the picket lines.

Unfortunately, the federal government did not take kindly to the labour unrest or any of the activities surrounding the strikers. On June 21, 1919, the Royal

Northwest Mounted Police charged into the large crowds demonstrating in the streets. Two men were killed and 100 wounded.

As for Helen Armstrong, she was arrested and spent four days in jail. Her husband George, one of the "Famous Ten" arrested for organizing the strike, served a year in prison. During his incarceration, Helen continued to agitate for worker's rights while providing for their four children. Thanks to the efforts of the Trades and Labour Council, of which Helen was the only female delegate, Manitoba eventually adopted a minimum wage in 1921.

Western Labor News, May 31, 1919 (Page 4)

NO NEED TO HUNGER

The Women's Labor League is doing splendid work through their restaurant adjoining the Strathcona Hotel. Hundreds of free meals are suplied there daily. No one need want.

This institution is receiving fine financial support from individuals and organizations and is well able to carry on.

Strikers, get your meals at the Labor League Restaurant. If you can pay for them do so. If you can't you are welcome.

This is the biggest thing in town today.—Real Brotherhood.

Calgary, May 29—Plumbers, Steamfitters and Teamsters joined strikers today. Miners say they are prepared for a three month's strike. All Calgary postal workers have been notified that they are dismissed. Freight Handlers, Clerks and Baggemen also line up with strikers.

Solidarity!

Conversion Charts

Temperatures

Gas Mark	F	°C
	32	0
	50	10
	100	40
	122	50
	212	100
1	275	140
2	300	150
3	325	160
4	350	180
5	375	190
6	400	200
7	425	220
8	450	230
9	475	250

Liquid Measures

Unit		fl oz	ml
teaspoon	1/3 tbsp.	1/5 fl oz	5 ml
dessertspoon	2 tsps	2/5 fl oz	10 ml
tablespoon	3 tsps.	3/5 fl oz	15 ml
cup	scant 1/2 pt.	8 fl oz	225 ml
breakfastcup	1/2 pt.	10 fl oz	285 ml
fluid ounce	2 tbsps	1/20 pint	28 ml
1 pint	2 cups	20 fl oz	570 ml
gill	1/4 pint	5 fl oz	140 ml
quart	2 pints	40 fl oz	1136 ml
1/2 pint	1 cup	10 fl oz	285 ml
1/4 pint	1/2 cup	5 fl oz	115 ml
2 pints	1 quart	40 fl oz	1136 ml
1 litre	4 1/2 cups	scant 2 pts	1000 ml
gallon	4 quarts	8 pt	4560 ml

Dry Weig	
Imperial	Metric (exact)
1/8 oz	3.5g
1/4 oz	7 g
1/2 oz	14 g
1 oz	28 g
2 oz	57 g
3 oz	85 g
4 oz	113 g
5 oz	141 g
6 oz	170 g
7 oz	198 g
8 oz	226 g
9 oz	255 g
10 oz	283 g
11 oz	312 g
12 oz	340 g
13 oz	368 g
14 oz	396 g
15 oz	425 g
1 lb	453 g
1 1/2 lb	680 g
2 lbs	900 g
2 1/2 lb	1134 g
2.3 lb	1 kg

Recipe Index

Recipe Index (continued)

Favourite Recipes

Photo Credits

Page 12 Ogilvie Flour Mills, 1905. Ogilvie's Book for A Cook, Montreal, QC: Ogilvie Flour Mills.

Page 15 Archives of Manitoba, Winnipeg — Buildings — Business N5174, Ogilvie Mill 1, c. 1885, Photo by Hall & Lowe.

Page 18 Archives of Manitoba, Lorene Squire Photographs, Ready to prepare the year's first meal of blue geese, 1939, H4-125-1-1.

Page 21 Archives of Manitoba, Humphrey Lloyd Hime collection, [BirchC39 box 1 photo 17 Bark tents, west bank of Red River, Middle Settlement] "Ojibway tents," September — October 1858.

Page 23 Lake of the Woods Milling Company, 1915. Five Roses Cook Book. Montreal, QC: Lake of the Woods Milling Company.

Page 24 Dick Thorsteinson private collection, New Iceland.

Page 26 Dick Thorsteinson private collection, New Iceland.

Page 28 Lake of the Woods Milling Company, 1915. Five Roses Cook Book. Montreal, QC: Lake of the Woods Milling Company, front cover.

Page 30 Lake of the Woods Milling Company, 1915. Five Roses Cook Book. Montreal, QC: Lake of the Woods Milling Company, p. 36.

Page 32 Dick Thorsteinson private collection, New Iceland.

Page 38 Joyal-Tellier family collection, Louis, Aurel, and Emile Delisle at the Delisle Bakery, St. Norbert, c. 1921.

Page 40 Archives of Manitoba, Arthur M. Irvine Fonds, HB2012/1, 2012/1/94, Lower Fort Garry, Manitoba, 1919, H4-183-1-1.

Page 43 (top) Archives of Manitoba, Hudson's Bay House Library photograph collection subject files, 1987/363-N-41.1/1-20 Norway House — Store Interior, ca. 1910, H4-191-3-5. Page 48 Musée St. Boniface Museum, DO-1224, The Recipe for the St. Lukes Organ Fund, Henderson Brothers, Printers, Winnipeg, 1910, RES. B-ET-24-C-9.

Page 44 Archives of Manitoba, Jessop Collection, Item Number 83, Girl and Eggs, 1916, Negative 3131.

Page 52 Archives of Manitoba, Peter Rindisbacher Watercolours, Buffalo, between 1821 and 1823, B22, Box 1.

Page 54 Archives of Manitoba, Foote Collection, Item Number 464, Immigrant Family, c. 1915, Negative 2064.

Page 56 Archives of Manitoba, H. Letourneau Collection, Pigeon Lake Farm and Red River Cart, Pigeon Lake, circa 1890, Item Number 4. Negative 17321.

Page 59 Archives of Manitoba, Red River Settlement, Métis Cottage — Homes 1, 1870, N4611.

Page 62 Archives of Manitoba, Personalities Collection — McClung, Nellie, Item Number 1, Negative 7694, Photo from Trail Magazine, December 1910.

Page 64 (top) Joyal-Tellier family collection, St. Norbert market-gardener Emile L. Joyal (right) off to market. Left of wagon, son Aurélius and daughter, Victorine, c. 1931.

Page 64 (bottom) Centre du Patrimoine, A. Gendreau- C. Bartmanovich Fonds, Laporte General Store, av de l'Église, St. Norbert, c. 1913.

Page 66 Manitoba Legislative Library, RBC, JV-60 Im6, Fruitful Manitoba, 1892, Box 5.

Page 70 Archives of Manitoba, Agricultural instruction posters, GR 8299, Immigration — Cream Grades, 1916-1921, D94-113.

Page 72 Oseredok, The Ukrainian Cultural and Education Centre, Ukrainian-English Cook Book, n.d., Winnipeg, MB.

Page 76 Musée St. Boniface Museum, DO-1224, The Recipe for the St. Lukes Organ Fund, Henderson Brothers, Printers, Winnipeg, 1910, RES. B-ET-24-C-9.

Page 80 Archives of Manitoba, George Harris Fonds, 1992-104, Plains Cree family Western Manitoba, c. 1900, C86/328.

Page 82 Centre du Patrimoine, Alida Laporte Gendreau et Claire Gendreau Barmanovich Fonds, Nurse Winnifred Grice, c. 1906, SHSB 33019.

Page 84 Oseredok, The Ukrainian Cultural and Education Centre, Ukrainian Cook Book, Ukrainian, European and Canadian dishes, Fourth Edition.

Page 88 Archives of Manitoba, R.T. Chapin Collection, New Year's Feast at John Monias, c. 1925, Item No. 129.

Page 90 Archives of Manitoba, Personalities — Guttormsson, Guttormur J. at the Ramsay Grave.

Page 92 (top) Archives of Manitoba, L.B. Foote fonds, Foote 1544, Royal Alexandra Hotel, August 4, 1922, P7399.

Page 92 (bottom) Archives of Manitoba, L.B. Foote fonds, Foote 1546, Kitchen, Royal Alexandra Hotel, March 17, 1944, P7399.

Page 94 Dick Thorsteinson private collection, New Iceland.

Page 96 Dick Thorsteinson private collection, Winter fishing camp, New Iceland.

Page 98 Dick Thorsteinson private collection, New Iceland.

Page 100 Dick Thorsteinson private collection, New Iceland.

Page 102 Archives of Manitoba, Jessop Collection, 65, N. Fehr Farm, Gladstone, 1916, N3116.

Page 104 Dick Thorsteinson private collection, New Iceland.

Page 107 Archives of Manitoba, George Harris Fonds, 1979-141, Album 14 page 37. "Red River Settlement House, Kildonan Park," 1919, P7451.

Page 108 Archives of Manitoba, Stores, St. Boniface, c. 1900, Number 10 , N17327.

Page 110 Archives of Manitoba, Mennonites 26, 1955, East Reserve, Mennonite home built 1885, Bergfeld, N29053.

Page 112 Centre du Patrimoine, Le Manitoba, le 21 mars, 1899, p. 15.

Page 114 Dick Thorsteinson private collection, New Iceland.

Page 117 Oseredok, The Ukrainian Cultural and Education Centre, Ukrainian Cook Book, НОВА КУХНЯ, p. 125.

Photo Credits (continued)

Page 118 Archives of Manitoba, Henry W. Jones photographs acquired by the Hudson's Bay House Library, 1987/250/N87 Woman, children around fire "under a wigwam frame," between 1905-1915, H4-198-3-1.

Page 120 Centre du Patrimoine, Gaston Bohémier Fonds, Josephine Grégoire Bohémier personal recipe collection, Lorette, 1408.

Page 123 Joyal-Tellier family collection. Joyal family garden in St. Norbert. (L-R) Emile, Corine, Sydonie, Aurélius, Victorine and Irène. Young Victorine, in front, 1908.

Page 125 Centre du Patrimoine, A. Gendreau-C. Bartmanovich Fonds, General Store — Z. Laporte, St. Norbert, 1915.

Page 126 Centre du Patrimoine, Gaston Bohémier Fonds, Josephine Grégoire Bohémier personal recipe collection, Lorette, 1408.

Page 128 Winnipeg Chinese Cultural and Community Centre Photo Collection, Sam Dong, c. 1924, Moon Dong.

Page 130 Blue Ribbon Manufacturing Company, 1905. Blue Ribbon Cook Book for Everyday Use in Canadian Homes, 16th edition. Winnipeg, MB: Blue Ribbon Manufacturing Company.

Page 131 Blue Ribbon Manufacturing Company, 1905. Blue Ribbon Cook Book for Everyday Use in Canadian Homes, 16th edition. Winnipeg, MB: Blue Ribbon Manufacturing Company.

Page 132 Oseredok, The Ukrainian Cultural and Education Centre, Ukrainian Cook Book, НОВА КУХНЯ, p. 125.

Page 136 Dick Thorsteinson private collection, Bakka 2nd house pre 1910, New Iceland.

Page 140 Archives of Manitoba, George Harris Fonds, 1979-141, Album 14 page 80. "Ruthenian Thatched Buildings, near Frazerwood," August 1937, P7451.

Page 142 Archives of Manitoba, Jessop Collection, Threshing time, 1916, N4029.

Page 145 Archives of Manitoba, W. J. Sisler, 201, Carrying milk or cream to the railway station at Malonton, N9628.

Page 146 Dick Thorsteinson private collection, New Iceland.

Page 149 Archives of Manitoba, W.J. Sisler Collection, Item Number 190, Ukrainian women picking cabbages, East Kildonan, 1916, N9603.

Page 150 Dick Thorsteinson private collection, New Iceland.

Page 153 Dick Thorsteinson private collection, New Iceland.

Page 154 Musée St. Boniface Museum, DO-1556, E.W. Gillett Co. Ltd., Magic Cook Book and Housekeepers Guide, Toronto, Winnipeg, Montreal: E.W. Gillett, cover.

Page 160 Musée St. Boniface Museum, DO-1224, The Recipe for the St. Lukes Organ Fund, Henderson Brothers, Printers, Winnipeg, 1910, RES. B-ET-24-C-9, p. 17.

Page 165 Lake of the Woods Milling Company, 1915. Five Roses Cook Book. Montreal, QC: Lake of the Woods Milling Company.

Page 166 Dick Thorsteinson private collection, New Iceland.

Page 168 Chef, Good Things and How to Cook Them, 1900, Toronto:
    Zam-Buk Company.
Page 169 Lake of the Woods Milling Company, 1915. Five Roses Cook
    Book. Montreal, QC: Lake of the Woods Milling Company.
Page 174 Centre du Patrimoine, Alida Laporte-Gendreau et Claire
    Gendreau Bartmanovich Fonds, 1906, Family dinner, St. Norbert,
    SHSB 30652.
Page 182 Archives of Manitoba, Mennonites 32, 1955, East Reserve,
    Mennonite home built 1885, Bergfeld.
Page 185 Blue Ribbon Manufacturing Company, 1905. Blue Ribbon Cook
    Book for Everyday Use in Canadian Homes, 16th edition. Winnipeg,
    MB: Blue Ribbon Manufacturing Company.
Page 186 Lake of the Woods Milling Company, 1915. Five Roses Cook
    Book. Montreal, QC: Lake of the Woods Milling Company.
Page 196 Archives of Manitoba, Jessop Collection, Children and
    berries, 1916, N4029.
Page 205 Archives of Manitoba, W. J. Sisler 115, Ukrainian farm,
    Fraserwood, Manitoba, 1914, N9606.
Page 206 Centre du Patrimoine, Le Manitoba, le 21 mars, 1899, p. 15.
Page 210 Dick Thorsteinson private collection, New Iceland.
Page 212 Dick Thorsteinson private collection, New Iceland.
Page 214 Archives of Manitoba, Jessop Collection, 69, Farm garden
    in Gladstone, 1916, N31120.
Page 224 Archives of Manitoba, Jessop Collection, Children eating
    bread and jam, 1916, N4026.
Page 227 Archives of Manitoba, L.B. Foote Fonds, Winnipeg General
    Strike crowd at Portage and Main, June 21, 1919, P7400.
Page 229 "No Need to Hunger," Western Labor News, May 31, 1919, p. 4.

About the Author

Christine Hanlon has a passion for food, people, and their stories. Her newest book Out of Old Manitoba Kitchens captures the essence of the province's rich culinary traditions, melding recipes, photographs and narratives of its earliest cooks, including the Indigenous people, Selkirk Settlers and first homesteaders. The co-author of The Manitoba Book of Everything spent many years penning articles for local and national magazines, on anything from homebuilding to restaurants. A regular judge at the Gold Medal Plates Canadian Culinary Competition, she lives in Winnipeg where she enjoys writing, entertaining, and, of course, cooking for family and friends.